Jenny Haberer

Sustainable Development Research

An analysis of determining factors for responsible environmental behaviour in regard to 'Solar powered Schools for Hyderabad'

Emerging megacities
Dicussion Papers
Edited by Konrad Hagedorn, Christine Werthmann, Dimitrios Zikos, Ramesh Chennamaneni

Humboldt-Universität zu Berlin
Department of Agricultural Economics
Division of Resource Economics
Philippstr. 13, House 12
10115 Berlin

Tel.: +49 (0)30 2093 6305
Fax: +49 (0)30 2093 6497
www.agrar.hu-berlin.de/struktur/institute/wisola/fg/ress
www.sustainable-hyderabad.de

Contact: emerging.megacities@hu-berlin.de

The emerging megacities discussion papers are available at:
www.eh-verlag.de

ISSN print edition 2193-6927

Emerging megacities Discussion Papers are prepared by researchers working on topics in the realm of sustainable development in Megacities of Tomorrow, a research priority by the German Ministry of Education and Research (BMBF). The papers have been peer-reviewed by a board of external reviewers.
Views and opinions expressed do not necessarily represent those of the Division of Resource Economics.
Comments are highly welcome and should be sent directly to the authors.
We welcome contributions on any topics related to Megacities of Tomorrow. Further information on the submission procedure is given at:
www.sustainable-hyderabad.de/emerging-megacities

Haberer, Jenny

Sustainable Development Research
An analysis of determining factors for responsible environmental behaviour in regard to 'Solar powered Schools for Hyderabad'

Emerging megacities Discussion Papers, Volume 8/2010

ISBN/EAN: 978-386741-825-6

First published in 2012 by Europaeischer Hochschulverlag GmbH & Co KG, Bremen, Germany.

© Europaeischer Hochschulverlag GmbH & Co KG, Fahrenheitstr. 1, D-28359 Bremen (www.eh-verlag.de). All rights reserved.

Cover: Photo "Metropolis", ferendus (flickr). Creative Commons License

No part of this publication may be reproduced or transmitted, in any form or by any means, electronic, mechanical, photocopying, recording or otherwise, or stored in any retrieval system of nay nature, without the written permission of the copyright holder and the publisher, application for which shall be made to the publisher.

EHV

Sustainable Development Research
An analysis of determining factors for responsible environmental behaviour in regard to 'Solar powered Schools for Hyderabad'

Jenny Haberer[*]

October 2010

Abstract

The underlying purpose of this paper is to analyse determining factors of responsible environmental behaviour, which serves as a formative evaluation prior to implementation of a pilot project with the aim of assisting the sustainable development of Hyderabad. This comprises the objectives of discussing the project strategy and aims, as well as analysing the target audience's individual behaviour and conditioning factors deriving from the external situation that require consideration in the design of the project's implementation strategy. A further implication is to clarify how present theories help to understand factors inhibiting or enabling responsible environmental behaviour and to provide knowledge on communication campaigns and strategy design.

The key findings indicate that theory on individual behaviour change from psychology and social studies is vast, however strategy designers of environmental campaigns do not make sufficient use of it and often develop programmes based on simplistic knowledge-attitude-practice models. On the other hand, literature on external factors determining environmental behaviour is not as advanced, besides the fact that a change of situational terms and conditions is postulated to yield great results. In general, individual and contextual factors need to be addressed to bring about the desired behaviour change, which has been considered in the strategy design of the 'Solar powered Schools for Hyderabad' project.

Key words: *sustainable development, climate change, communication, environment, responsible environmental behaviour, education, communication campaigns, behaviour change, solar power, Megacity, Hyderabad, India*

---

[*] Email: jenny.haberer@gmail.com, nexus - Institute for Cooperation Management and Interdisciplinary Research GmbH, Otto-Suhr-Allee 59, Berlin

Introduction

Climate change today is a reality caused by people, affecting people and an issue that can only be solved by people. Partly, it is the result of an approach to economic growth and development that has proven to be unsustainable.

A country that has marked accelerated economic growth in the past decade is India (2007-2009 CAGR 7.5 %) – the largest democracy in the world with a population of 1.15 billion (World Bank, 2009a). India's integration into the global economy has brought economic and social benefits; however, the development has also given rise to problems. One of the major challenges is the continuing spread of urban development. In 2009, 29.8 % of the total Indian population were urban citizens. The metropolitan areas of India today are bursting at the seams, stressing infrastructure, resources such as housing, education and transport, as well as the ecological system, due to expanding energy and resource consumption and constantly increasing greenhouse gas emissions.

This is an indication that a long-term growth is only sustainable if city attributes, such as pollution, congestion and safety are improved alongside urban economic development (Gill and Kharas, 2007 cited in Chetan, 2009). Unambiguously, the rapid growth of metropolitan areas necessitates environmental planning, which includes strategies to reduce CO_2 emissions.

Hyderabad, the state capital of Andhra Pradesh, is an emerging megacity in Southern India, which is estimated to have a population of 10.5 million by 2015.

In order to allow for a sustainable development of Hyderabad, the Federal Ministry of Education and Research (BMBF) Germany, in cooperation with the Indian government, has initiated the 8-year development project "Hyderabad as a Megacity of Tomorrow", with the aim of designing a "Perspective Action Plan" that will establish Hyderabad as a "Low Emission City in Asia" in 30 years time (BMBF, 2010). To achieve this vision researchers are developing adaptation strategies and pilot projects. "Solar powered Schools for Hyderabad" is one of the pilot projects the nexus Institute is dedicated to. The project aims at achieving outcomes across a number of sectors: social, ecological, educational, physical, economic, and political, as well as outcomes at the cognitive individual behaviour, community and systems level. At the school level the objectives are to increase energy supply, and thus improve learning conditions, while at the same time fostering awareness on alternative energies and low emission lifestyles. This particular objective as part of the project builds the focal points of this discussion.

Over the last decades research by psychologists and sociologists has concentrated on exploring the factors which influence environmentally friendly action in order to improve environmental education and communication programs. Earlier research on environmental behaviour has focused on the hypothesis that knowledge, attitudes and behaviour are linked in a linear model, and, even though today it is known that this proposition is incomplete, many development programs still design their strategies based on this concept. Yet, environmental communication involves much more than simply conveying information to a neutral audience. A wide array of internal (knowledge, attitudes, beliefs, norms, etc.) and external factors (institutional, economic, social, cultural, etc) determining behaviour, need to be taken into consideration when promoting environmental behaviour change (Steg & Vleg, 2008).

The process of designing respective campaigns includes thorough formative evaluation, which provides information on the current situation, the target audience, including an analysis of their present behaviour and their beliefs about the proposed behaviour, as well as an investigation of communication mechanisms that people use to adopt responsible environmental behaviour.

Therefore, the research question of "Which factors facilitate or prohibit responsible environmental behaviour with regard to the 'Solar powered Schools for Hyderabad' project?" constitutes the cornerstone for this study.

Moreover, the findings that will shape the discussion of the research question will be derived at by addressing the following objectives:

1. Determination of theoretical background from literature on characteristics and strategy of the 'Solar powered Schools for Hyderabad' project

2. Identification of efforts undertaken by local actors to promote pro-environmental behaviour in children

3. Analysis of the level of knowledge, awareness and behaviour of children from secondary schools on environmental issues and low-emission lifestyles prior to project implementation

To start with, it is important to know to which extent theories from the spheres of social science, psychology and communications specifically addressing environmental awareness and behaviour, provide insights into topic related issues, such as: What is the definition of environmental friendly behaviour? Which factors determine behaviour change? How can these factors be measured? And what implications are proposed by literature for the strategy development of communication campaigns? This will be assessed in Chapter 1.

Thereupon, the 'Solar powered Schools for Hyderabad' project will be discussed in detail from an analytical and strategic perspective in Chapter 2. A description of the project background and situational factors that led to the formation of the project is followed by the presentation of aims, objectives, target group and the overall theory of change underlying the pilot project.

Chapter 3 attempts to identify actors and their communication strategies on promoting responsible environmental behaviour in children from secondary schools in Hyderabad. First insights into the Indian secondary school system will be provided in order to analyse institutional factors that have an effect on children's behaviour. Moreover, the role of non-governmental organisations that have introduced many initiatives and policies to advocate environmental education will be assessed. This chapter therefore aims at learning from communication mechanisms that are currently employed, as well as identifying opportunities of coalition for the pilot project.

In Chapter 4 the question will be what internal factors determine environmental behaviour. Results from a quantitative study aim at characterising the target audience in terms of their knowledge, beliefs about environmental issues as well as their present behaviour. To fulfil this objective a conceptual model including particular variables for measurement was designed based on knowledge generated from the literature review.

Finally, the gathered findings relating to the three objectives are compiled and discussed in regard to insights from theory in order to find an answer to the research question.

Consequently, the implications of this study are twofold. The study aims to derive a guideline or key factors that ideally will be considered in the design of the 'Solar powered Schools for Hyderabad' project for promotion of environmental awareness and low-emission lifestyles, by the nexus Institute. Moreover, the implication is to apply current knowledge from literature, academics and secondary data to a specific case and examine to what extent the aim of the study can be reached or which limitations exist by doing so.

Methodology

Social research aims at exploring reality and understanding human behaviour and actions. Moreover, it offers the basis to suggest possible solutions to social problems. A variety of methodologies and methods are employed in social research, since it is diverse and pluralistic (Sarantakos, 2005). Babbie (2007, p. 297) likewise states: 'Evaluation research refers to a research purpose rather than a specific method'. It is defined as the process of determining how social interventions can produce envisaged result or whether specific activities have led to the desired outcome (Babbie, 2007). This can be done with various research methods. Academics distinguish between two main areas of research, namely quantitative or qualitative.

Quantitative research is chosen when the need to systemise easily quantifiable data exists. Quantitative research is perceived in an instrumental way, where, based on clear and objective facts, numerical data is collected and mathematical and statistical tools are used to evaluate the findings (White, 2002). The mathematical and objective nature of quantitative research can accord for greater accuracy of results and simplifies comparability with other studies. It aims at discovering, explaining and documenting general causal laws, by studying and learning about social events. This technique is limited in that research is often conducted in an unnatural environment in order to gain a certain level of control over the subject, leading in some cases to superficial datasets. It strictly relies on methods, predefined research concepts and their results. Consequently, findings might not match real world results nor reflect how people really feel about the exercise (Learn Higher and MMU, 2008b).

The second type of research method, the *qualitative study* is a descriptive, non-numerical way to collect and interpret information. This method is preferred when investigating a phenomenon of which there is little knowledge (White, 2002). It contains elements from various schools of thought and the findings can provide a rich, detailed picture about, for example, attitudes, feelings and behaviour of people. The research takes place in actual and everyday settings and the researcher is often part of the research. The latter gives ground to the main criticism raised by opponents who neglect this method due to its subjective nature (Babbie, 2007). Moreover it is said to be limited in efficiency, due to the lack of studying relationships between variables accurately, so as to derive at knowledge about social trends or to establish social policies.

The research design underpinning this paper incorporates a combination of qualitative and quantitative approaches to data collection. According to the objectives of the study the relevant research methods are explained.

Primary research questions:

- What theoretical background does literature provide in relation to characteristics and strategy of the 'Solar powered Schools for Hyderabad' project?
- What efforts are undertaken by local actors to promote pro-environmental behaviour in children?
- What is the level of knowledge, awareness and behaviour of children from secondary schools on environmental issues and low-emission lifestyles prior to project implementation?

As such the first question serves to obtain background information and a general understanding of the project. Findings from questions two and three aim at identifying which factors promote or inhibit responsible environmental behaviour. Ideally the results will be incorporated in the design of the implementation strategy of the project.

First, literature primarily in the fields of social psychology, responsible environmental behaviour, communications and social development was reviewed, with the aim to place the 'Solar powered Schools' project into a theoretical framework and to learn what research results from other studies suggest in terms of factors determining responsible environmental behaviour.

1. Solar powered Schools for Hyderabad

In respect to the objective of presenting the strategy and characteristics of the 'Solar powered Schools for Hyderabad' project, qualitative research was conducted. Key informant interviews with the project leaders and analysis of secondary data provided by the project team generated the case related findings on project aims and objectives, target group, project partners and background information on schools, education and energy issues.

2. Promotion of pro environmental behaviour in Hyderabad

Next, in order to investigate the efforts undertaken by local actors to address environmental issues in Hyderabad, desk research accounted for insights on the Indian school system and the state of environmental education, as well as the identification of main organisations and their strategic approaches in promoting responsible environmental behaviour.

Moreover, primary data was gathered by conducting semi-structured expert interviews with three interview partners. First, the interview with De Paul Kannamthanam, one of the founders of Yardstick, a private organisation promoting experimental learning, helped in gaining an understanding of the education system in India (Appendix 1). Second, Minhajuddin Farugi, an independent environmental consultant who worked for 6 years at the Centre for Environment Education (CEE), gave insights into the state of environmental education in India, the work of CEE and challenges in the field (Appendix 2). And third, W.G. Prasanna Kumar, the director of National Green Corps (NGC) for the Hyderabad region, a non-profit organisation working towards environmental conservation, provided detailed observations into the work of the organisation and an opinion on various strategic directions employed by NGC and other organisations (Appendix 3). Interviews were conducted by the author of this study in Hyderabad. The conversations were audio-taped and notes taken during the interview process. The use of extended questioning and discussion with a free flow of response generated important findings. A transcript from the interview was sent to the respondents to make sure all statements were fully understood and not misinterpreted in any way.

Additional information on CEE was gained through an e-mail interview with the CEE program coordinator for the Hyderabad region, Vanitha Kommu (Appendix 4). In cases where a personal interview is not possible, distant interviews are an eligible tool to access information from respondents (Gillham, 2007).

And finally, a three-day workshop (12.-14. May 2010) at the World Wide Fund for Nature (WWF-India), where the author facilitated youth from Hyderabad, provided additional findings on the work of this organisation. This research method can be categorised as participant observation from the sphere of ethnography (Geertz, 1973), as it included a close and intimate involvement with people and their practices in their natural environment over a period of time.

The combined approach of primary and secondary data collection was found to be an effective method to meet the second objective of providing general background information of present programs and strategies by actors addressing environmental issues in Hyderabad.

3. Environmental knowledge, awareness and behaviour

Research objective three aims at identifying cognitive (e.g. knowledge, action skills) and affective (beliefs, feelings, emotions) factors determining pro environmental behaviour in the individual.

For this purpose a quantitative research approach was chosen, employing a survey design in the form of a paper-based, self reported questionnaire (Appendix 5). The literature review in conjunction with insights from the expert interviews mentioned afore provided the baseline for the design of the set of questionnaire items.

Since the 'Solar powered Schools for Hyderabad' project envisages fostering awareness and low emission lifestyles, the front-end evaluation in form of a survey attempts to measure environmental behaviour-related variables. The intention is, for one, to understand the current level of awareness and behaviour and second, to investigate possible causal relationships of how one variable precedes another and brings about changes in the other variable.

The literature review enabled the development of an applicable conceptual model combining the variables up for discussion. A description of the survey procedure, participants, the conceptual model and the specific variables under investigation will be presented in Chapter 4 after establishing the logical connection through the findings in the literature review.

Limitations in quantitative research method

The applied research method is constrained by limitations.

First, by conducting a survey, data can be gathered in a fast and simple way. However, the analysis is based on a small sample size only, which is not truly representative for the whole population.

Second, investigations of phenomena that involve beliefs, feelings, attitude and behaviour are commonly undertaken through qualitative research. Anthropologists criticise the use of quantitative surveys in this sphere, since the predetermined questions concerning minimal units of complex variables, asked in a standard fashion, can by no means be organised into a profound system towards understanding the cultural beliefs and a reasonable description of the way people think and act (Pelto & Pelto, 1997). However, it is acknowledged that surveys do permit a systematic comparison of behaviour-related variables, by statistical analysis of relationships. This can help in deriving knowledge about social trends or in establishing social policies.

1 Literature Review

1.1 Responsible Environmental Behaviour Theories

Changes in human behaviour are believed to be needed in order to tackle problems, which pose a threat to environmental sustainability. The answers to the questions: 'Why do people act environmentally and what are barriers to pro-environmental behaviour?' are extremely complex.

Responsible environmental behaviour (REB) is defined by Sivek & Hungerford (1989-1990, cited in Cottrell & Graefe, 1997) as "any individual or group action aimed to do what is right to help protect the environment". The array of issues studied in relation to promoting environmental behaviour change is vast, and covers internal factors (motivation, knowledge, belief, attitude, awareness, norms, responsibilities and locus of control) and external factors (institutional, economic, social and cultural factors) (Steg & Vleg, 2008).

1.1.1 Internal Factors

Many of the theories focusing on the individual imply that people make reasoned choices.

Early approaches to promote REB were concerned with raising environmental awareness and concern by linking knowledge to attitude. These models assumed education was the key to success. However, in practice this attempt proved incomplete. The hypothesised liner relationship between knowledge and attitude ignores the myriad of psychosocial variables that influence behaviour. Quantitative research has shown that there is a discrepancy between attitude and behaviour. These studies also showed the difficulty in designing valid studies to explain this gap (Kollmuss & Agyeman, 2002; Rodrigues, 2007).

Theory of Reasoned Action/ Theory of Planned Behaviour

One of the most influential attitude-behaviour models stemming from socio-cognitive psychology is Ajzen's and Fishbein's *Theory of Reasoned Action* and *Theory of Planned Behaviour*.

The *Theory of Reasoned Action (TRA)* model is composed of two primary constructs: attitudes and subjective norms. *Attitude* is the person's overall positive or negative evaluation of performing the behaviour (based on beliefs and expected outcome), whereas *subjective norm* refers to the person's perception of social pressure to perform (influenced by normative beliefs and motivational factors). According to the authors these two constructs affect the formation of *behaviour intention*, which is the person's motivation or goal-oriented decision to perform the behaviour and is the immediate antecedent for actual *behaviour (Ajzen & Fishbein, 1980)*. As such, attitudes do not determine behaviour directly, but in conjunction with social norms they influence behavioural intentions. The ultimate determinants of any behaviour are the behavioural beliefs.

In 1985 the theory was expanded by the addition of one further predictor of behaviour intention and renamed *Theory of Planned Behaviour (TPB)* by Ajzen himself. The new variable is 'perceived behaviour control', which derives from Bandura's (1977) concept of Self-Efficacy and refers to a person's perceived control over the ease or difficulty of performing the behaviour, determined by factors such as motivation, outside sources of persuasion, prior success in performing the task, and feelings of frustration associated with repeated failures. (Langdridge, Sheeran & Connolly, 2007; Bandura, 1977 cited in Abram, 1989).

Ajzen's and Fishbein's Theory of Planned Behaviour is one of the most frequently cited and applied models in environmental behaviour research (Bamberg & Möser 2006; Cottrell & Graefe, 1997; Kaiser, Oerke & Bogner, 2007; Kollmuss & Agyeman, 2002; Ohtomo & Hirose, 2007; Steg & Vleg, 2008).

Model of Responsible Environmental Behaviour

In 1986, Hines, Hungerford and Tomera (cited in Bamberg & Möser, 2007) published their *Model of Responsible Environmental Behaviour* which was based on the TPB. Similar to the TPB, intention to act is a direct determinant of REB, and can be used when it is not possible to measure revealed behaviour. In turn, the intention to act is influenced by a combination of cognitive and affective factors.

Cognitive factors are related to knowledge of environment including abstract knowledge (knowledge of issues) and concrete knowledge (knowledge of action strategies and action skills). *Abstract knowledge* is considered an important variable for the entry level, when the respondent is largely unaware of environmental issues. *Knowledge about skill and action* is considered an important variable for the empowerment level (Hwang, Kim & Jeng, 2000).

Affective factors concern the feelings or emotions associated with the objects and are generally defined by attitude, locus of control and personal responsibility. *Attitude* is considered as one of the most important influences on behaviour (Ajzen & Fishbein, 1980). Hines et al. (1986 cited in Weidenboerner, 2008) found that many researchers used basically two types of attitudes about environment: attitude toward ecology and environment as a whole, and attitude toward taking action. The factor *locus of control* equals Bandura's (1977 cited in Abram, 1989) concept of efficacy and includes both internal and external dimensions. External locus of control is based on the belief that changes happen by chance or by the intervention of powerful others such as god or the government rather than by personal behaviour. One who has stronger external locus of control is therefore not likely to participate in activities to bring about change. In contrast internal locus of control is an internal motive that leads to the expectation that one's own activities are likely to bring about change.

A person with strong internal locus of control is more likely to participate in the behaviour. With reference to *personal responsibility*, Hines et al suggested that a person who has more individual interest in a certain issue is more likely to invest resources in it and thus has a higher responsibility to act (Hwang, Kim & Jeng, 2000).

One significant difference to the TPB is that the model of predictors of environmental behaviour considers situational factors (economic constraints, social pressure, and opportunities to chose different actions) to have a major influence on actual behaviour, in addition to intentions, as can be seen in Figure 1.

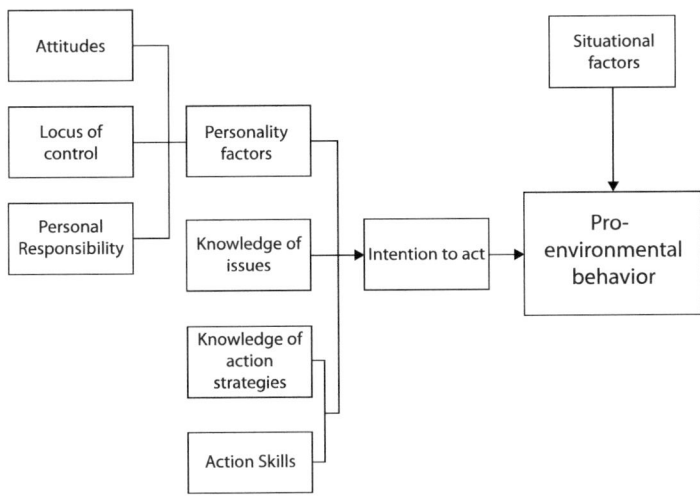

Figure 1: Model of predictors of REB
Source: Hines et al., 1986 adopted from Kollmuss & Agyeman, 2002

The study undertaken by Hines, et al. exerted a strong impact on the continuing research on psycho-social determinants of REB (Bamberg & Möser, 2007).

Further models relating to internal factors

A number of studies (Homburg & Stolberg, 2006; Story & Forsyth, 2008) attempted to explain REB in response to problem focused-coping, which is determined by demand (threat, harm) and resource (efficacy) appraisals, stemming from the *Protection Motivation Theory* proposed by Dr. R.W. Rogers in 1975 (cited in Maddux & Rogers, 1983). According to the theory we protect ourselves based on two factors: threat appraisal and coping appraisal. The threat appraisal refers to a person's perceived severity or harm stemming from a situation. With reference to environmental protection, Story & Forsyth state that individuals will not take action to address environmental problems if they never notice that the environment is threatened. As such the threat appraisal is an indicator for environmental awareness. The coping appraisal is a combination of the concept of self-efficacy (Bandura, 1977 cited in Abram, 1989) and response efficacy (the perceived effectiveness of the behaviour recommended to remove the threat or harm). According to Rogers these factors influence the decision on whether to act or not. It is postulated that a higher perception of threat and as such a higher concern for the environment, as well as a higher belief in one's ability to cope with an issue are associated with higher REB (Maddux & Rogers, 1983). Homburg and Stolberg (2006) likewise conclude that appraisal processes activate problem-focused coping, which in turn leads to REB.

Numerous attempts have been undertaken in order to identify variables which close the gap between attitudes and environmental behaviour through factor analysis. Wiseman and Bogner (2003 cited in Oerke, 2007) criticise the various approaches for being insufficiently tested on reliability and validity. Their *Model of Ecological Values (2-MEV)* is two-dimensional and encompasses two attitude scales: preservation (biocentric viewpoint: having an appreciating relationship with nature) and utilisation (anthropocentric viewpoint: man over nature). According to the authors attitude can be conceptualised as a behaviour antecedent by these two scales (Oerke, 2007).[1]

The few studies presented, relating to internal factors affecting REB, could only provide a small insight into the research field. They all involve rather different antecedents of environmental behaviour and the portrayed perspectives proved to be pre-

---

[1] A number of independent cross-testing studies agreed with the findings (Boeve-dePauw, Donche & VanPetegem, 2010; Milfort & Duckitt, 2004; Oerke, 2007 cited in Bogner 2010).

dictive of at least some types of environmental behaviour. However, as yet it is not clear which perspective is most useful in which situation.

Moreover, they all implied that people make reasoned decisions, which stems from the psychological school of cognitivism. In behaviourism, in contrast, human behaviour is seen as definite, and the important role of environmental factors in the formation of behaviour is recognised (Abram, 1989).

1.1.2 External Factors

Learning Theory

One of the primary representatives of the behaviourists is Burrhus Frederic Skinner (1957, cited in Mills 1998), who devised the *learning theory*[2]. The foundational thinking of this theory stems from evolutionary psychology and is based on the fact that higher organisms show spontaneous behaviours. The research focuses not only on the behaviour itself, but also on the circumstances that accompany the behaviour. There are two factors in which behaviour is influenced by the environment, for one through incidents preceding the behaviour and second through consequences that follow the behaviour. An important aspect therefore is the notion of 'control'. It is assumed that the environment 'controls' behaviour in some way or the other and that behaviour can be influenced or changed by variation of terms under which the behaviour occurs. According to the learning theory complex behaviour is learned gradually through the modification of simpler behaviours. Imitation and reinforcement play a crucial role here. The theory states that individuals learn by duplicating behaviours they observe in others and behaviour changes occur through rewarding 'good' behaviour or punishing 'bad' behaviour (Mills, 1998; Bördlein, 2009; Steg & Vleg, 2008).

Unintentional decision making

In relation to environmental behaviour, Ohtomo and Hirose (2007) investigated the decision making process by considering unintentional decision making in regard to situational factors. They tested the reactive process based on prototype image (mental image of the typical person engaging in socially undesirable behaviour) and descriptive norm (to what extent the socially undesirable behaviour prevailed amongst close peers). It was found that the reactive process may lead to acceptance of eco-unfriendly behaviour and that attitude-behavioural studies may falsely constrain possible explana-

---

[2] Besides Skinner, other important and noteworthy researchers influencing behaviour theory are: Ivan Pavlov, Edward Lee Thorndike and John B. Watson (Mills, 1998)

tions encompassing the influence of situational factors which are not directly related to eco-friendly goals or reasons.

A further model highlighting the importance of situational factors, besides internal factors in promoting behaviour change is the Elaboration Likelihood Model, which has only limited predictive value but finds widespread practical application.

Elaboration Likelihood Model

The *Elaboration Likelihood Model (ELM)* proposed by R.E. Petty and J.T. Cacioppo (1981, 1986, cited in Petty, Briñol & Tormala, 2002) refers to how attitudes are formed and changed through persuasive communication.

According to the theory, the route to persuasion is dependent on a person's elaboration level. Elaboration pertains to the extent to which a person thinks about the issue and about relevant arguments contained in a message. There are two routes to persuasion: the central route where the audience considers the idea logically by drawing on knowledge and experience, and the peripheral route which is characterised by using contextual elements, relying on incidental cues such as credibility or attractiveness of source, to process the message. In general, more effort is devoted to understanding matters if motivation is high, implying the issue is of personal interest and relevance, including a feeling of accountability and personal desire to consider this issue. Moreover, the individual needs the ability to be persuaded, which is dependent on the subject's general education level, and cognitive resources (presence or absence of time, pressure, distractions, etc.).

A quintessential proposition from this theory is that attitude formation depends on contextual factors and settings (Griffin, 2006; McQuail, 2010; Petty, Briñol & Tormala, 2002).

Contextual factors in regard to REB

In the discussion about environmental behaviour Steg & Vleg (2008) highlight the importance of considering contextual factors such as physical infrastructure, technical facilities, availability and characteristics of products and legal frameworks, as they may facilitate or constrain environmental behaviour. For example, legal regulations could be altered in order to penalise bad behaviour or reward environmentally friendly behaviour. Moreover, financial policies could be used in order to decrease prices of pro-environmental products or raise prices for environmentally less friendly alternatives. However, changes resulting from modifying conditions, circumstances or the context have not been examined systematically or monitored over time by researchers.

It was found that rewards are more effective than sanctions in encouraging proenvironmental behaviour. However, rewards tend to have an effect only as long as the reward is in place and as long as they make pro-environmental behaviour more attractive than environmentally harmful options. For example, policies promoting the adoption of energy efficient equipment are preferred over policies aimed at reducing existing equipment (Geller, 2002; Poortinga et al., 2003; Steg et al. cited in Steg & Vleg, 2008). Moreover, it is hypothesised that sanctions may initially reduce people's quality of life perceptions, but after a period of adjustment, sanctions are accepted and in fact have not reduced the quality of life by any significant degree. Actual effects may differ from pretested perceptions and acceptance; yet resistance should not necessarily be an indicator for not implementing a policy (Tretvik, 2003 cited in Steg & Vleg, 2008). There is still a large gap in knowledge about contextual factors of environmental behaviour; especially the role of various rewards and punishments needs further scrutiny, besides increasing general understanding about how contextual factors affect various environmental behaviours (Steg & Vleg, 2002).

1.1.3 Encouraging pro-environmental behaviour

Geller (2002, cited in Steg & Vlek, 2008) identified four key issues for encouraging pro-environmental behaviour: (1) thorough selection of the behaviours to be changed to enhance environmental quality, (2) analysis of causes of those behaviours, (3) application of adequate intervention to change relevant behaviours and their antecedents, and (4) methodical evaluation of effects originating from those interventions on the behaviours themselves.

First, it is important to select factors, which have a significant negative environmental impact, assess the feasibility of behaviour changes and identify specific groups to be targeted. Second, in practice, the challenge lies in identifying specific barriers that hinder pro-environmental behaviour.

Third, the identified predictors of REB need to be translated into strategies resulting in actions. Even though research has shown that an increase in knowledge and awareness does not lead to REB, many actors encouraging pro-environmental behaviour continue to develop education programs and communication strategies based on such simplistic assumptions (Kollmuss & Agyeman, 2002). Steg & Vleg (2008) argue that the effectiveness of behavioural intervention generally increases when they are aimed at both: antecedents of the relevant behaviour (internal factors) and at removing barriers for change (external factors). However, they also point out that structural strategies are probably more effective in promoting pro-environmental behaviour than are informational strategies. And fourth, intervention needs to be systematically evaluated before and after the implementation, concentrating on aspects such as relevant behaviour changes, predictors of behaviour, environmental quality, and individual quality of life (Steg & Vleg, 2008).

1.2 Communication for Change

When it comes to real life practices of behaviour change all intervention approaches have one thing in common: they use communication as a tool for addressing social problems, partnering with communities and engaging people in understanding and solving social issues. Therefore, communication is an integral part of any social change strategy.

The term communication has been interpreted in many different ways. In the sociopsychological tradition of communication theories the emphasis lies on finding cause-and-effect relationships within a framework of '*who* says *what* to *whom* through what channel and with what *effect*' (Lasswell, 1984 cited in McQuail, 2010). Based on this framework, research focused to a large extent on investigation of factors influencing the effectiveness of persuasive communication and exploration of how change (effect) is influenced by the source of message (who), the content of the message (what) the audience's characteristics (whom) and the chosen medium of communication (channel) (Ajzen & Fishbein, 1980; Griffin, 2006).

1.2.1 Public Communication Campaigns

A wide-spread approach for the application of intervention aimed at behaviour change is via public communication campaigns. Coffman (2002) provides the following definition: "Public communication campaigns use the media, messaging, and an organised set of communication activities to generate specific outcomes in a large number of individuals and in a specified period of time". Even though aspects of communication campaigns vary across categories, researchers distinguish broadly between two main types, depending on the primary purpose of the campaign: *individual behaviour change campaigns* versus *policy change campaigns*.

Individual Behaviour Change Campaigns

Individual behaviour change campaigns are also called public information campaigns or education campaigns. Objectives of such campaigns include influencing knowledge and beliefs about behaviours, affecting support of behaviour through attitude change and persuasion, the ultimate purpose being a decrease in individual's practices causing social problems or the promotion of behaviours which bring about improved individual or social well-being. As such, individual behaviour change campaigns can be seen as rather informational, since they do not change the external context. Particular segments of the population are the target audience of these social marketing campaigns, which employ a variety of strategic tools, be it the commercial sector, public relations, marketing or advertising. Psychological studies, as discussed above, provide the basis on how to bring about and measure behaviour change, and campaign designers and evaluators should make use of this knowledge (Coffman, 2002).

Policy Change Campaigns

Policy change campaigns on the other hand are concerned with structural spheres, changing circumstances under which behavioural choices are made, aiming finally at mobilising public and decision maker support for policy endorsement or change.

These campaigns focus on creating public will in order to legitimise the importance of a social problem in the public domain with the aim to motivate public officials to take policy action and bring about policy change (Henry & Rivera, 1998 cited in Coffman, 2002).

Figure 2 shows Coffman's model of the general theory behind policy of change campaigns. It is acknowledged that the model does not represent the only theory of change; rather it resembles a composite sketch of important factors showing the flow from campaign activities towards the ultimate outcome by depicting common types of variables and their relationship.

The basic theory of change that underlies most policy change campaigns encompasses media, the public and policy agenda setting, in this particular order (Bohan-Baker, 2001a, cited in Coffman, 2002). These campaigns attempt to start up a chain reaction in the agenda-setting process, based on the fact that many people develop their opinion about a social issue through the media, and what the public thinks, cares about and does will have a significant influence on the policy agenda. Hence, a bilateral approach is taken by working to affect what is on the media's agenda and how issues get reported (media advocacy & coverage) and by communicating directly to the public (message dissemination & public will generation). Typically the communication activities are accompanied by other activities, such as coalitions with institutions, network building, policy maker outreach or community organising.

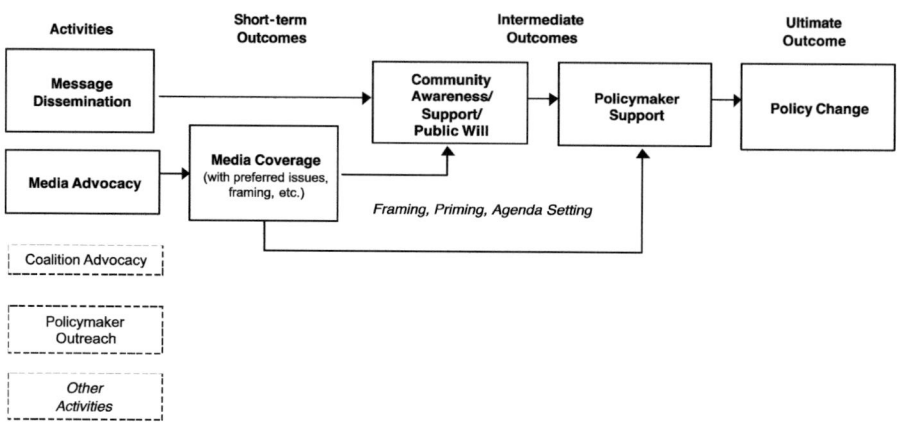

Figure 2: Theoretical Model of Policy Change Campaigns
Source: Adopted from Coffman, 2003

The media assumes a prominent position in models of policy change campaigns as well as behaviour change campaigns, since it is common to many communication efforts working toward change.

There are three core communication concepts of how the media influence public or individual opinion.

(1) Agenda Setting: the process of placing issues in a particular volume on the policy agenda for public consideration and intervention, (2) Framing: the way a story is told – its selective use of particular symbols, metaphors and messengers, which in turn has an influence on how people interpret the issue and make sense of it for themselves, and (3) Persuasion: the ability to recognise and manipulate attitudes.

An important difference between agenda-setting and persuasion is that persuasion tends to focus on those people with the specific problem and rely strongly on behaviour theories, while agenda-setting attempts to influence media portrayals of a group and its social issues with the focus on elected officials who have the power to change the problem through the process of media advocacy (McQuail, 2010).

1.2.2 Communication towards Community Change

Today, it is commonly known that a variety of development projects failed soon after implementation because the target groups were not involved. It is argued that media advocacy and policy agenda setting with local elites, without involving the grassroots population to bring about social change and development, resembles the old dominant paradigm of the trickle-down approach. "People's participation *is becoming* the central issue of our time." (Diouf, 1995:8, cited in Moemeka, 1997) Destructive ethnocentricity needs to be avoided. Instead of throwing information at people and talking at people we need to learn to communicate with them and talk with them, listen to their views. We need to get to know the audience and the socio-cultural context (Moemeka, 1997). Therefore, a key feature of development programmes has been the recent effort to decentralise planning and implementation, with local communities being mobilised to take greater control and ownership of the programmes.

Coffman (2003) likewise highlights that recent approaches deliberately use a public will and an individual change component in conjunction and as such the characteristics of both campaign types can be overlapping. Affecting public will can also be an element of behaviour change campaigns, as well as vice versa, in which communication efforts geared towards policy change might include elements in their design, which build awareness and affect attitude at the grassroots level. Researchers and policy makers have to figure out where the locus of responsibility for the behaviour change should be. Is the desired outcome in the realm of personal or public behaviour?

Social Diffusion

One influential representative of the humanistic and personal perspectives to development and social change was Everett Rogers, the author of the classic diffusion of innovation model (1995). According to Rogers an innovation is an idea, concept, object or actual practice which is regarded as new by an individual or social group and diffusion is the social process by which the innovation is communicated over time among the members of a communication network or within a social sector.

Social diffusions can be considered as a special type of communication process which deals with the question of how new ideas spread throughout society (Rogers, 2001 cited in Rodrigues 2007).

The diffusion of new ideas encompasses four main elements: (1) the innovation, (2) the social system within which the process takes place, (3) the required adaptation time and (4) the communication channels used for the dissemination of the idea.

(1), (2) Rogers identified five key characteristics which work in favour of disseminating the innovation within a particular social system.

Relative Advantage is the degree to which the new idea is perceived as better than the existing idea. It is considered as the single most important motivating factor for change within the target group.

Compatibility refers to the consistency of the new idea with the target group's needs and sociocultural context. This means providing alternatives which are valid within the system and consistent with fundamental and basic beliefs.

Complexity addresses the level of difficulty involved in understanding and implementing the idea. Structure, language and procedure appropriate to the target group are necessary for the simplification of the idea.

Trial-ability is concerned with the extent to which the idea can be implemented on a trial basis. Target groups are known to have a greater appeal to innovations which have been tested in their social context. A visible success of a trial project helps to build up people's confidence.

Observability refers to the degree to which immediate and longitudinal results of an innovation are visible to others.

(3) In sum, the greater the relative advantage of the new idea, its compatibility, observability and trial-ability, and the lesser the complexity, the more rapid the idea will be adopted (Moemeka, 1997; Rodrigues, 2007; Rogers, 1995).

(4) The communication channel is the means by which the new idea gets disseminated from one individual to another. This could be communication through mass media (see earlier: media concept of persuasion) or through interpersonal channels, which are more effective in forming and changing attitudes toward a new idea, according to Rogers (1995). We decide to adopt a new idea for ourselves, after asking the opinion or observing the behaviour of someone whom we know, trust or consider an expert; these are the 'opinion leaders'. The social influence of opinion leaders is what drives the diffusion and leads to adoption of the idea by followers (Rogers, 1995).

1.2.3 Evaluation of public communication campaigns

While there is a great pool of research on theory, methods, outcomes, measures and evaluation tools of individual behaviour change, there is far less understanding of the same factors in the area of public will and policy change campaigns. Many campaigns aim simultaneously at environmental change (public policy, agenda setting), community level change (affecting norms, expectations, and public support), and individual behaviour change (skill teaching, positive reinforcement, and rewards), which make evaluation of the initiatives difficult.

Coffman (2002) presents four types of evaluation. The first type is *formative evaluation*, which is conducted 'front-end', before and during the implementation of the project. Information collection on questions such as what is the current situation, what does the target audience think about the issue, and what messages and messengers work best, help to shape the design of the campaign. The other three types are 'back-end' evaluations. *Process evaluation* measures the effort and the direct outputs of the campaign, how the activities involved are working, but it does not capture the campaign's effects, which is the aim of *outcome evaluation*. Here, the emphasis is on determining if the campaign's objectives have been met, such as measuring change in knowledge, beliefs, attitudes and behaviour. The last type, *impact evaluation*, measures the achievement of long-term aims. It is usually more resource-intensive and expensive to conduct, but it yields the most accurate answer to the question of whether the campaign produced its intended outcomes.

Front-end evaluation is important for the design of the campaign, but also provides the opportunity to establish baseline measurements for back-end evaluation. As such all four types need to be well coordinated as they are interlinked.

1.3 Key Findings from Literature Review

The question of 'what are the barriers to REB, how to identify, measure and remove them' has been studied by many researchers from different fields. A great deal of the studies focus on internal factors, and researchers agree that environmental knowledge, attitude and awareness are only indirectly linked to REB. However, in practice, addressing these factors is still the main objective for environmental activists when designing their strategies. Creating REB is much more complex and needs to take additional factors into consideration. Bogner's (2003 cited in Oerke, 2007) 2-MEV model for example suggests that environmental attitude is determined by values (preservation vs. utilisation),

Homburg & Stolberg (2006) emphasise the importance of problem-focused coping, referring to the threat appraisal, and the Model of Responsible Environmental Behaviour (Hines, Hungerford & Tomera, 1986 cited in Bamberg & Möser, 2007) considers social norm, self-efficacy, personal responsibility, as well as situational factors.

Situational factors play an important role in unintentional decision making, and the descriptive norm or prototype images have been studied in this context and found to have an influence on REB (Ohtomo & Hirose, 2007). Moreover, Petty & Cacioppo's ELM (1981,1986 cited in Petty, Briñol & Tormala, 2002) suggests that contextual factors are vital for a person's elaboration level and need to be considered in the attempt to promote REB. In their conclusion Steg & Vleg state that focusing on both internal and external factors (institutional, economic, and political) generally increases the effectiveness of REB interventions, yet strategies aimed at structural changes might yield better results. This implies that communication efforts need to be both politically and psychologically effective.

Policy change campaigns, for example, are based on structural strategies. Their ultimate outcome is a policy change toward REB, which can be achieved through community organising and mobilising combined with media advocacy. Media advocacy and policy maker outreach alone, however, are perceived to be insufficient. Involving the local community from which opinion leaders will emerge, who can communicate the new idea as to its relative advantage, compatibility, trial-ability and observability, as well as reducing the fear of complexity, is crucial in propagating the idea of REB. Bringing about individual behaviour change and front-end and back-end evaluation of the intervention strategy, should employ knowledge from psychological studies.

Having established the theoretical background for the research, in the following three chapters findings for the research objectives will be presented, leading up to the discussion of determining factors for environmental responsible behaviour in respect to the 'Solar powered Schools for Hyderabad' project.

2 Definition of theoretical context for the Solar powered Schools project

2.1 Project Background

Since 1997 India's economy has registered an average growth rate of more than 7 %. The strong economic development is accompanied by large levels of migration from rural to urban areas. In 2001, 27.8 % of the total Indian population were urban citizens, which in numbers constitutes 285 million people. By 2026 the urban population is expected to rise to approximately 38 %.

In general, there is strong empirical interdependency between the index of city liveability and a nation's GDP per capita. This indicates that long-term growth is only sustainable if city attributes, such as pollution, congestion and safety are improved alongside urban economic development (Gill and Kharas, 2007 cited in Chetan, 2009).

"The sustainable development of the Megacities of Tomorrow" with a focus on "energy- and climate efficient structures in urban growth centres" is one of the major research tasks of the Federal Ministry of Education and Research (BMBF), Germany. Under this umbrella, one of the projects undertaken in cooperation with the Indian government is "Hyderabad as a Megacity of Tomorrow". The aim of the 8-year research and development program is to design a "Perspective Action Plan" that will establish Hyderabad as a "Low Emission City in Asia" in 30 years time (BMBF, 2010).

Hyderabad, the state capital of Andhra Pradesh, is the sixth largest metropolis in India, with six million inhabitants. By 2015, it is estimated, Hyderabad will be holding rank 21 in the list of world's largest cities, with a population of 10.5 million, and hence will be a future megacity[3] (Spreitzhofer, ca. 2006). The emerging megacity experiences rapid economic growth enabling higher living standards and modern lifestyles for the emerging middle class. Hyderabad's shift towards a modern consumer society has led to a growth in commercial energy and indirect energy uses, e.g. of energy embodied in products and services. Consequently, modernisation, urbanisation and lifestyle change processes are accompanied by constantly increasing per capita greenhouse gas emissions.

Climate change effects in the region are already present: severe floods in 2002, strong heat waves in 2003 and altogether three drought years between 2000 and 2007 have caused serious damage to the economy and human life, of which one third is currently living below the poverty level and suffering from severe food and health problems. "These new issues arise while the old problems are still unresolved" (Hagedorn, 2006).

Responding to the anticipated climate change impact and contributing to the resolution of the arising problems is what numerous actors in the project are committed

---

[3] **Megacities** are urban agglomerations with more than 10 million inhabitants, (UN, 2003), which fall among this category based on their size (quantitative definition). They are predominantly located in third world countries (Exception: Tokyo/Japan). Megacities are often so called primacy cities, which means they fulfil highly concentrated administrative, economic, social as well as cultural and scientific functions. Therefore, they bundle a major aggregation of power and have a high influence, especially within their nation's borders (Spreitzhofer, ca. 2006).

to doing, by exploring greenhouse gas mitigation and adaptation strategies and designing pilot projects under the core hypothesis "getting the institutions right"(Hagedorn, 2006). One of the pilot projects within the nexus work package 'Communication and Participation Strategies for Low Emission Lifestyles' is called "Solar powered Schools for Hyderabad" and constitutes the focus of this discussion.

Research results and previous activities of the project team with local partners (workshops, field-trips, etc) provide support for a project dealing with the relation between energy and lifestyle.

The current energy distribution and consumption patterns in Hyderabad are perceived as having significant negative environmental impacts. The following is a rough outline of contextual and individual factors indicating unsustainable behaviour in relation to energy.

Contextual factors

On the supply side, Andhra Pradesh's energy system suffers from many failures and is highly insufficient, which fosters the already existing gap between energy demand and supply. Also, electricity generation in Hyderabad is heavily reliant on thermal (coal & gas) sources of energy, which is very carbon intensive. Renewable energy accounts for no more than five percent of Andhra Pradesh's electricity, besides the fact that especially solar energy has tremendous potential in India with 250-300 sunny days a year (nexus, 2010a). Solar energy has the estimated physical potential for 94 % of India's additional electricity needs by 2030, which can leapfrog grip extension (depending on the application it can be used on or off grid), thus eliminating transmission and distribution losses and can contribute to national energy security (Harris-White, Rohre & Singh, 2009). A detailed discussion about the current state of solar technology, institutions and politics would clearly exceed the scope of this study, yet a few words on the topic should be mentioned. Harris-White, Rohre & Singh (2009, pp. 56, 57) provide an insight into existing hurdles: "The right technology is available and is not obstructed by patent law so much as by the structure of domestic subsidies, the reluctance of banks, [and] price instabilities [...]. The wrong choices are locked-in to India's energy system through the non-transparent, lifecycle and lifetime physical and financial requirements of fossil fuel [and nuclear] technologies competing for public support and infrastructure."

A step in the right direction is the Jawaharlal Nehru National Solar Mission (2009), which is part of India's National Action Plan on Climate Change. It is a recent effort to promote ecologically sustainable growth by setting up an enabling environment for solar technology, in particular aiming to support entrepreneurs and creating interest in the investor community, as well as establishing conditions to drive down costs toward grid parity[4] (nexus, 2010a). Most people in the industry believe that once grid parity is reached, demand for photovoltaic products will increase significantly. This, however, implies that consumers are aware of the sustainable energy solution in their city and its benefits over traditional power (Frontiers, 2005).

Individual factors

On the demand side energy consumption patterns at the top end of the income distribution scale produce CO_2 approaching those of North America (Harris-White, Rohre & Singh, 2009). In the peri-urban areas households have no or only an unreliable energy supply, thus the use of traditional biomass for fuel (e.g. firewood) is high – a sources of energy which contributes significantly to increased amounts of greenhouse gases in the atmosphere, adding to global warming. The gap between power demand and supply increases the number of scheduled and unscheduled power cuts and fluctuations which affects all sectors of society (nexus, 2010a).

According to Harriss-White, Rohra & Singh, 2009 the 'social' status of renewable energy in India is low and the diffusion about solar energy is slow. For one this is due to the fact that most households can not afford the initial high cost of solar installation, provided that they are even aware of this alternative source of energy. In addition, social movements in India have been dominated by issues relating to gender, poverty and ethnic groups, and only recently the environment has come into focus. However, the role of energy, and solar in particular in the environmental movement is not significant. Moreover, a content analysis of print media, a primary source of information for Indian's on aspects relating to climate change, revealed that media frames the topic in a manner where the focus is put on threats of climate change and its causes. The latter is attributed to the 'advanced economies', which are being demanded to lead the way out of the problem (Harriss-White, Rohra & Singh, 2009).

The nexus institute interprets the limited public interest in climate change as a result of how the issue is communicated. Currently, communication efforts seem to be dominated by knowledge generation employing scientific abstract concepts, yet ignoring the link between the phenomena and affects on people's livelihoods. The local context, as well as activities to foster environmental protection, which are seen as crucial in generat-

---

[4] **Grid parity** is the point at which alternative means of generating electricity is equal in cost, or cheaper than grid power (Frontiers, 2005).

ing public interest and promoting local action at the individual level, is missing (nexus, 2010a).

2.2 Pilot Project - Solar powered Schools for Hyderabad

In consideration of the discussed factors, a respective action plan has been developed. The overall aim is to implement pilot projects at the community level dealing with alternative energy, and utilising the learning and outcomes from monitoring and evaluation of those projects to establish strategies for participation and corporation with the industry and policy makers.

Target group

Field trips revealed that there is a high interest in a pilot project dealing with alternative energy at the school level. There are a number of schools in Hyderabad that have an insufficient or unreliable energy supply. In a growing economy, education plays a key role and shapes future development. Therefore good learning conditions have to be assured. Moreover, the school system provides the largest organised base for environmental education and action. School children in particular are an important target group within the community for achieving a sustainable development, and especially in this case for raising environmental awareness and promoting the adoption of low-emission lifestyle practices. Children are still open for changing their behaviour and can function as opinion leaders. Consequently, three secondary schools and one education institute form the target group of the project.

> The focus of this study lies on the three differing secondary schools. One school is located in the slum area of Hyderabad, in an environment where economic poverty, poor hygiene and sanitation highly affect the community. The second school is the Sri Aurobindo International School. This school is affiliated with the ICSE board[5] of education and is actively working towards the overall development of children by employing progressive approaches to learning. The final school is the Muslim IQRA Mission High School, lying in a part of the old city of Hyderabad, which is still registered as a slum area. The secondary branch of this school follows the SSC[5] board and is environmentally active (nexus, 2010b).

The assumption that changes in behaviour are essential to cope with the implications of climate change in the region is the basic component of the project. As identified in the literature review, the first step toward encouraging behaviour change, prior to strategy design, is the thorough selection of the behaviours to be changed to enhance environmental quality (Geller 2002, cited in Steg & Vlek, 2008).

Behaviours to be changed

It is envisaged that the installation and use of the solar panel becomes an integral part of the schools, in a way that they are fully self-managed. This requires that it will be included in the teaching and curriculum, which will generate knowledge and awareness in students and teachers of the application's relative advantage and compatibility, as well as an understanding and hands-on experience on what can be done to live environmentally responsible.

Moreover, the installation should be made visible and the focus of discussion in the local community and press in order to generate public interest. In this instance the school will act as an opinion leader, communicating the feasibility and benefits of using alternative energy as well as the importance of low emission lifestyles.

Thorough monitoring, evaluation and recording of the findings will be required in order to have a sound baseline of the showcase for the intended capacity building and policy outreach activities.

Intended outcomes

The project aims at achieving outcomes across a number of sectors: social, ecological, educational, physical, economic, and political (horizontal complexity), as well as outcomes at the cognitive individual behaviour, community and systems level (vertical complexity).

- Provision of a sustainable, environmentally sound solution, for closing the gap in the school's energy supply and making them energy self-sufficient (ecological)
- Better learning conditions for the children through energy security (physical)
- Fostered awareness of alternative energies and low emission lifestyles at school and community level (social, educational)
- Triggered diffusion of alternative energies in the local community (ecological, economic)
- Learning from implemented programs for an understanding of possible institutional and organisational solutions, as well as feasible and effective policies and technolo-

gies towards increased energy efficiency and promotion of renewable energy in the Hyderabad region

The overall theory of change including the strategy and aims of the project are visualised in Figure 3. As can be seen in the figure the ultimate outcome of the project aims at policy change, yet it is not merely a policy change campaign, but contains an integrated individual behaviour change campaign with intervention towards REB at the school and community level. To achieve this aim the project team requires a strong network of partners from various sectors, such as local technology suppliers, non-governmental organisations active in the environmental movement and media partners for capacity building.

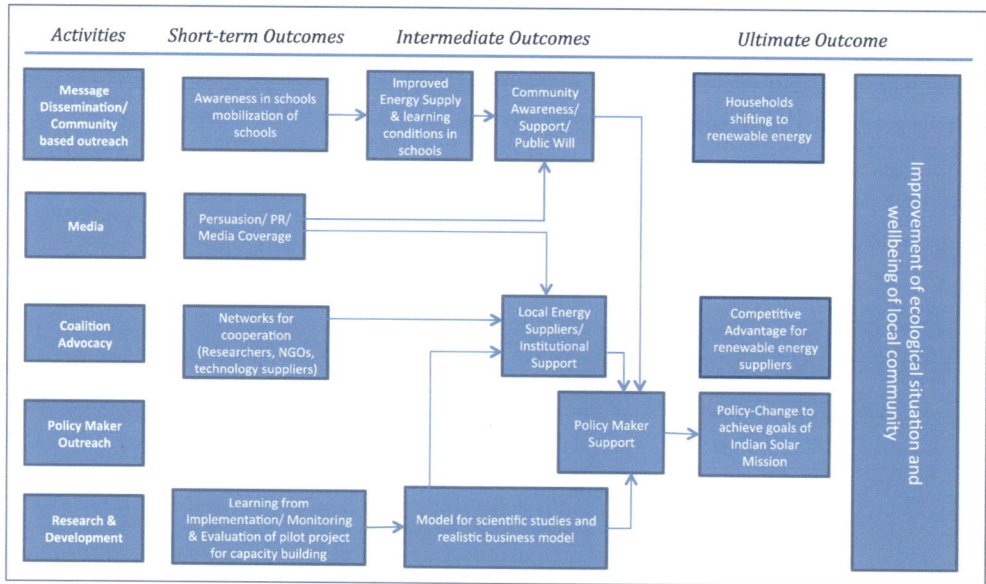

Figure 3: Theory of Change for 'Solar powered School for Hyderabad' project
Source: Figure developed by the author of this study, based on a model adopted from Coffman, 2003

Proceeding from here the research will now concentrate on the individual behaviour change at school level and deal with the primary research question of this study, one of the key issues of encouraging pro-environmental behaviour: 'Identification of factors determine the relevant behaviour'. In order to derive an answer for which factors encourage or prohibit the behaviour, research question two will be addressed: 'What efforts are undertaken by local actors to promote pro-environmental behaviour in children in

Hyderabad?'. Moreover, this exercise aims at identifying opportunities for coalition building.

3 Encouragement of REB in children by local actors in Hyderabad

3.1 Secondary education

Secondary education in India is institutionally diverse. There are different kinds of secondary schools, which can be distinguished according to the management board they are affiliated to. Each board has its own specified curriculum and school certificate examinations. Schools are differentiated into public schools and types of private schools. The majority of schools in India are public schools affiliated to the according state government and comply with the board of Secondary School Certificate (SSC)[6]. The share of non-government schools in secondary education in Andhra Pradesh is 25 % (World Bank, 2003). Of the private schools, the majority are also affiliated to the SSC. A second type of private schools conforms to the Central board of Secondary Education (CBSE) which is associated with the National Council for Education Research and Training (NCERT). NCERT is the apex body for curriculum related matters for school education in India. Finally a third type of private schools follows the board and curriculum of the Indian Certificate of Secondary Education (ICSE). In the following the four school types explained will be referred to as government schools (the public schools), SSC schools, CBSE schools and ICSE schools.

The interview with Mr. Kannamthanam (Appendix 1), one of the founders of Yardstick, a Hyderabad-based private company with the mission of making learning an enriching and joyful experience, which they aim to accomplish by promoting hands-on learning (experimental learning) in science and mathematics, provides important insights into the characteristics of Indian secondary schools and the kind of education pupils receive in Hyderabad.

Yardstick was founded against the backdrop that proper assessment in Indian education is totally neglected. Children only generate knowledge from textbooks and learn by memorising, but practical learning is lacking. Simply restating scientific concepts won't

---

[6] A small fraction of the public schools, are central government schools, complying with the Central Board of Secondary Education (CBSE). [Commonly, children of citizens serving in the National Defence Force attend these schools].

make children understand nature. Only if they can discover and experience it, they will develop ownership and truly understand. Yardstick's approach is to use activities and experiments to demonstrate and enable discussion with the children. From his two-year work experience in the field Mr. Kannamthanam named a number of challenges the firm faces in promoting practical learning.

- First of all, in India in early ages a culture is created whereby children are discouraged from asking questions. This is problematic, since questioning is the key to understanding. Teachers themselves lack a lot of understanding, resulting from the way they were educated and trained. In hands-on learning a lot of questions emerge, which consequently challenges teachers and requires extra effort.

- In government and SSC schools extra effort is not rewarded. In the end teachers receive the same payment and respect or appreciation from the principal, as long as the syllabus is completed. In general, school management is open for change; the problem, however, is to motivate teachers to be part of it. The quality of teaching is not assessed. There is no control over teachers. They have a high work load, with tests every two or three weeks and administrative work- it is monotonous. As such teachers lack motivation; incentives are missing.

- ICSE schools have more practical application and a wider outlook for the all-round development of students. They offer many after school activities, e.g. sports or coaching for IIT. 'Every parent wants their child to be an IIT engineer'. Therefore, children face a lot of pressure from many sides.

- Lately CBSE has been stressing activity-based-learning and is in the process of establishing more practical learning techniques. This is new for the schools. The textbooks are quite advanced, but teachers have not been successful in adapting yet. Quantitative assessment and teaching by textbook is hard-wired, after years of employing this practice.

- There is high competition between schools, in terms of student's performance in examinations.

World Bank reports (2003, 2009) on secondary education in India further strengthen the arguments. A comparison of Indian and international curricula suggests that India is under-performing at the secondary level, and has scope for significant improvement in terms of access and quality of education. In public secondary education, which accounts for the majority of schools, the quality of instruction and learning is alarmingly low.

There is an over-emphasis on rote learning of facts as opposed to development of students' conceptual understanding and higher-order thinking skills. This is directly linked to the poor standards of teacher's education at the secondary level, which is characterised by outdated pedagogical approaches, inadequate provision of basic teaching and learning materials, weak accreditation and monitoring, and little incentives for improvement. The World Bank reports further that publicly financed secondary school teachers are largely unaccountable to parents, headmasters and educational administrators. A positive development was the design of the National Curriculum Framework (NCF) of 2005, which provides a set of guidelines for secondary education across the country aimed at improvements in the overloaded Indian school curriculum. However, the final decision on curricula content rests with the states and board. More efforts are needed to align state board curricula to the NCF, including financial incentives and technical assistance.

Table 1: Characteristics of schools across the different boards of secondary education

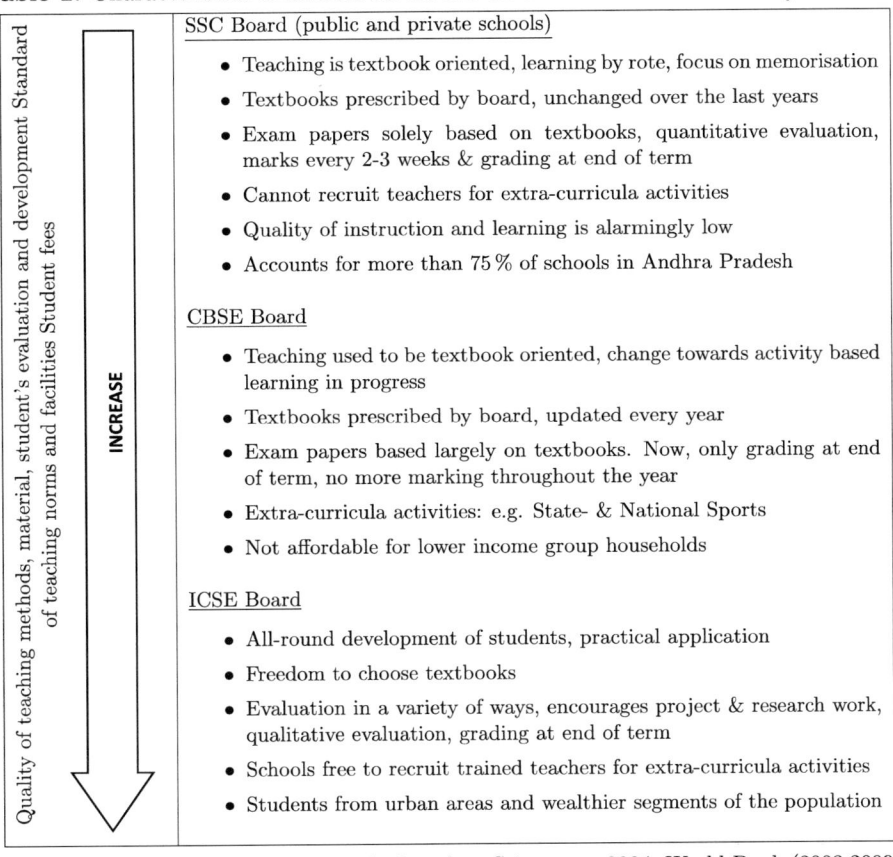

SSC Board (public and private schools)
- Teaching is textbook oriented, learning by rote, focus on memorisation
- Textbooks prescribed by board, unchanged over the last years
- Exam papers solely based on textbooks, quantitative evaluation, marks every 2-3 weeks & grading at end of term
- Cannot recruit teachers for extra-curricula activities
- Quality of instruction and learning is alarmingly low
- Accounts for more than 75 % of schools in Andhra Pradesh

CBSE Board
- Teaching used to be textbook oriented, change towards activity based learning in progress
- Textbooks prescribed by board, updated every year
- Exam papers based largely on textbooks. Now, only grading at end of term, no more marking throughout the year
- Extra-curricula activities: e.g. State- & National Sports
- Not affordable for lower income group households

ICSE Board
- All-round development of students, practical application
- Freedom to choose textbooks
- Evaluation in a variety of ways, encourages project & research work, qualitative evaluation, grading at end of term
- Schools free to recruit trained teachers for extra-curricula activities
- Students from urban areas and wealthier segments of the population

Source: Created by author of this study, based on Srivastava, 2004; World Bank (2003,2009); Kannamthanam, 2010 [Appendix 1]

Additional highlights of the report are that most secondary students are boys, and disproportionately from urban areas and wealthier segments of the population. Students from the poorer quintiles are unable to afford privately managed schooling and hence join the government system with its low quality.

For interventions at school level, it will be important to assist each school in conceptualising its own strategic plan for development. One factor for success will be a principal with a vision and ability to motivate teachers and parents. Intervention strategies would necessarily involve a complex and comprehensive approach that includes redesigning curriculum and textbooks, and training of teachers. The critical player is the teacher.

The Table 1 summarises the characteristics of the school types, providing important insights into the different education pupils receive in Hyderabad.

These facts are an indication for the hypothesis that the level of knowledge and the ability to understand and cope with such complex issues as climate change and sustainable development is significantly different across the school types.

3.2 Environmental Education in secondary schools

In spite of rapidly changing lifestyles the unified approach to protection of the environment is inherent in India's cultural and religious ethos which accentuates the interconnectedness between the natural environment and human life. It is against this backdrop that the country's environmental education strategy has emerged (Ravindranath, 2007; Roberts, 2009).

India's National Policy on Education (1986 cited in Sarabhain, approx. 2005) states: "There is a paramount need to create consciousness of the environment. It must permeate all ages and all sections of society, beginning with the child." Since then the Government of India, in partnership with educational institutions and various non-Governmental organisations (NGOs), has introduced many initiatives and policies to advocate environmental education (EE) in schools and colleges nationwide (Joshi, 2005).

In 1991 the Supreme Court of India directed all education departments in the country to make EE compulsory at all levels of education. Following this ruling, the Pune-based Bharati Vidyapeeth Institute of Environmental Education (BVIEER, 1999 cited in Roberts, 2009) did a two-year content analysis of textbooks, studying their handling of environmental content. The exercise revealed that while textbooks contain some environmental content, there are a number of 'gaps' that need to be addressed. Textbooks lack appropriate action links, they do not reflect local environmental issues adequately and there is "very poor infusion of information on sustainable lifestyles" in the EE curriculum. The exercise also helped to conclude that there is a need for revised curricula and teaching methodologies (BVIEER, 2002).

Based on these findings, textbooks have been redesigned and efforts have been made, both at the central and state level to integrate environmental related topics into the teaching of many subjects (Shet, 2003). The most recent National Curriculum Framework (2005) recommended infusing EE into different disciplines such as science, social science and languages. Consequently, EE is incorporated in various subjects in schools following CBSE. Under the SSC board environmental education is not compulsory, the extent of infusion is presumably less than in other schools. In ICSE, environmental education is a separate subject[7], delivered by a specified teacher trained in the field (Farugi, 2010 [Appendix 2]).

Per se EE is reasonably well anchored in school curriculum; however, it has not been coupled with appropriate changes in teacher education curricula, accounting for the time lag between policy generation and application to practice. The question arises if the complex, interrelated environmental themes find a sufficient place and time in the conventional subjects they are infused into (Ravindranath, 2007). Considering the above mentioned curriculum overload, problems reported by teachers are for example lack of time and resources, as well as lack of institutional and parental support, hindering an integrated action-focused approach at school or community level, as suggested by environmental education research (Shet, 2003). Environmental education needs learner-centred, explorative and problem solving teaching techniques, as opposed to the conventional practice of knowledge transfer on concepts of ecology and environment. However, the current teacher education system does not equip teachers with the necessary skills and competence to promote environmental issues and develop the right principles, values, skills and good practices in children that would lead to environmental awareness and sustainable action. Furthermore, it has been criticised that environmental education in India does not reflect local issues; the link to the needs and realities of the local community is missing. The necessary skills of organising field-based action need to be developed in order to build reciprocal links between school and community (Ravindranath, 2007).

The policy generation for introducing environmental education in the schools curriculum, entails a whole new set of skills and additional effort by teachers, giving them

---

[7] The ICSE board recognises that education for sustainable development needs a multi-disciplinary approach as opposed to a single discipline. Therefore, EE will be infused into various subjects, in two years time (From conversation with Environmental Education teacher at St. Ann's High School, Hyderabad, 2010).

an important role in contributing to sustainable development, which has not been accounted for sufficiently. Making environmental education work requires a whole-system approach and a broad base of support.

The support of local non-governmental organisations (NGOs) is vital in the development towards sustainability and responsible environmental behaviour. NGOs assist in the capacity building of communities towards achieving sustainable development by providing education, knowledge and skill. In fact, NGOs support the community in developing the resources, building awareness, motivating to participation in project and finally enhancing the quality of livelihood in a community (Nikkha & Redzuan, 2010).

3.3 Role of environmental NGOs

India has a very large number of NGOs in the environmental movement involved in activities as wide as India's biodiversity and natural habitat. Their activities include policy analysis and agenda setting, public awareness campaigns, field projects in urban and rural communities as well as school programs, training, research and documentation, just to name a few.

NGOs play a key role in both creating the conceptual and experiential basis of sustainable development, and act as opinion leaders in the country in the field (Joshi, 2005).

The conducted secondary and primary research revealed that there are quite a number of small and big players in the Hyderabad region focusing on youth involvement towards pro-environmental action. The following three have been identified as key actors, and hence will be discussed further: Centre for Environment Education (CEE) a governmental independent institution and National Green Corps (NGC) popularly known as a program of eco-clubs, both established by the Ministry of Environment and Forest (MoEF), Government of India, and the internationally active World Wide Fund for Nature (WWF).

Centre for Environment Education (CEE)
CEE was established in 1984 by the MoEF, yet is an autonomous body set up as an NGO, with the vision to play a leading role in generating awareness about nature and nature conservation (Sarabhai, approx 2005).

CEE's strategy is built on certain key concepts, namely a focus on people, flexibility in program and material design, partnerships, utilising complementary strengths and involving government organisations and NGOs in strategy development; achieving maximum reach and impact. Their goals are reflected in their pursuit of effective use of media and technology, facilitating networking through communication, building on experience and learning from others and having regional presence and international experience (Sarabhai, Raghunathan & Jain, 2002).

Over the years the NGO has created strong linkages between education, capacity building and field demonstration through partnerships with over 160 NGOs. Agenda setting towards policy change, field level activities, teacher training, textbook development and organizing workshops, discussions and exhibitions on education for sustainable development are activities CEE is involved in (Sarabhai, approx 2005).

Since the past ten years CEE has been working in Andhra Pradesh. Each CEE office is independently able to take decisions, collaborating with other offices when needed. The Andhra Pradesh team consists of 16 people, working on ongoing projects related to Environmental Education in Schools of Andhra Pradesh, water & sanitation, experiencing nature, awareness generation, environmental management of rural livelihoods and natural resource management with the help of local NGOs. Currently, government rural schools form the major target group since these schools cannot afford additional activities, like private schools can, and with the multiplier effect[8] the largest audience at school level will be reached (Kumma, 2010 [Appendix 4]; CEE, 2010).

The interview with Mr. Farugi (Appendix 2) revealed that CEE does not directly work with children, but focuses largely on teacher education, including material and resource development. The actual field work is done through local NGOs. The success of previous programs conducted at private schools was reported as being excellent, mainly due to the fact that once the principal understands the benefits of the actions, he/she will 'force' the teachers to implement them, which is not the case at government school level. Due to lack of control and monitoring, 'at government schools the result was practically zero.' Ms. Kumma equally reports that lack of motivation among teachers becomes a barrier, and that the schools require continuous guidance and monitoring, which is difficult due to time, budget and human resource constraints. Besides these institutional problems, the challenge lies in translating the relatively new, very scientific, complex and intangible topic of climate change and all its aspects into child friendly words. The topic requires larger publicity. On the positive side, CEE benefits from its partnerships, which enable the development of high quality material and result-oriented

---

[8] CEE demonstrates projects in samples at some government schools and it is been taken forward to multiple other schools with the help of NGOs and teachers.

programmes.

World Wide Fund for Nature (WWF)

WWF-India is the country's largest and oldest nature-conservation organisation. It is a non-governmental organisation with 60 % of its funding coming from voluntary donations by private individuals. WWF-India articulated its mission in 1987 as follows: "The promotion of nature conservation and environmental protection as the foundation for sustainable and equitable development." (WWF, 2010c)

The work of the formerly named World Wildlife Fund, used to focus specifically on species conservation, freshwater and wetland initiatives as well as forest management and conservation. Recently, the urgency of addressing climate change has been recognised, which led to the addition of 'reducing people's ecological footprint' to WWF's strategic goals, and commencement of diverse activities from education and capacity building, legal action, policy research and advocacy, campaigning and field conservation projects. Thereby the organisation can rely on its well established conservation alliances with business, trade and commerce and its long-standing experience in creating synergies with media. In recent years, mass communication has played an increasingly valuable role for WWF-India in achieving its goals, as well as creating brand awareness. Extensive media coverage, strong PR, use of new media, up-to-date web content and use of social networking sites were employed to communicate to the masses (WWF, 2010c).

Besides media communication, WWF-India regards education to be crucial in bringing about responsible environmental behaviour. 'Knowledge creates awareness, and the right attitude is the prerequisite for sustainable social action' (WWF-India, 2010a). Therefore, WWF-India employs an environmental education programme aimed at fostering REB in students, youth and communities alike. 20 schools from 10 cities, one being Hyderabad, participate in The 'Young Climate Savers' program, working towards sustainable school campuses by strengthening individual and institutional capacity. Activities undertaken include teacher training workshops, story telling, exhibitions, talks, competitions, field trips and film screening (WWF-India, 2010b).

The participatory observation undertaken during the three-day workshop at the WWF-India Andhra Pradesh office generated behind the scenes insights into a branch of this world-famous organisation. The Hyderabad-based team consists of Farida Tempal, the State Director and five employees. The education officer, Mr. Saravanan, reported that the target group for environmental education in schools is private schools, following CBSE or ICSE. At this point in time, the initiatives at school level as part of the 'Young

Climate Savers program' have a rather information-providing character, including material provision for teachers, presentations, talks and selection of students in charge who will ensure ongoing activities at the school. A clear challenge is a lack of human resources, which makes the effectiveness of monitoring and control activities more difficult.

At the beginning of the workshop, where the observation on WWF-India was conducted, the participating children were very enthusiastic about working with and learning about an organisation of such high reputation. Unfortunately, the employees were very time-constrained due to high workloads. Finally, the task given to the children for the three days was to create a presentation related to climate change, describing the topic and its aspects in a child friendly manner. At the end the children's initial enthusiasm had diminished; instead of gaining profound knowledge of the organisation and experiencing their work in the field, the children helped in material design used by WWF-India for promotion of sustainable development.

This is an indication for the challenge lying in communicating the complex topic effectively towards children, which also became evident in conversations with Farida Tempal, who confirmed this viewpoint. Additionally it was mentioned that time and human resource constraints are barriers to success. Facilitators for success are clearly WWF-India's strengths in having strong brand awareness, substantial media linkages and firm commercial alliances.

National Green Corps (NGC)

The National Green Corps (NGC) is a national programme across India conceptualised and initiated by the MoEF in 2001-02. Under the Environment Education and Awareness Scheme of the Ministry, so called Eco-clubs have been established in over 130,000 schools across the country to create environmental awareness among children. The programme aims at building a cadre of young green corps working towards environmental conservation (MoEF, 2010b). More specifically, the aim of the NGC is: "To impart environmental education and to encourage and mobilise participation of school children in various environment education activities in their localities" (MoEF, 2010a). Eco-clubs are run by teachers or a group of students who participate in the various activities that are assigned to them. They conduct a number of activities such as planting on the school campus, organising rallies, motivating others to keep the environment green and teaching them about conserving natural resources and saving electricity. Awareness about the dangers and causes of global warming is spread through puppet shows, debates and quizzes. A 2009 study by N.S. Roberts assessing the impact of eco-clubs revealed that the programme provides an educational forum for students who lack awareness. Effectiveness was judged as high, especially when the club cooperated with other NGOs and it was headed by active teachers-in-charge with a strong commitment. Otherwise, weaknesses of the programme are operational shortcomings, such as a need for better training of teachers, and a re-examination of the upper management and its vision is recommended. Apparently most objectives could not be met due to a lack of efficiency, overemphasis on quantity versus quality, and a lack of interest in the programme at school level. Moreover, success is not visible, and monitoring and evaluation are insufficient. In general, the concept is well laid-out and has led to raised awareness in schools having great interest, but there is scope for improvement.

The interview with Prasanna Kumar (Appendix 3), the state director of NGC for Andhra Pradesh was very informative and valuable, since he shared his experience from a quite self-critical standpoint. In Andhra Pradesh the NGC deals with 5,750 secondary schools of all types (government, SSC, CBSE, ICSE), which is a large number to manage for a team of five people. Based on the objectives of NGC, Mr. Kumar started with a strategy that focused on teacher training and material development aimed at knowledge creation and awareness building, which according to constructivist theory is the route to behaviour change. However, after ten years of working in the field he drew the conclusion that "Knowledge generates knowledge, only. Out of 5,750 schools I am dealing with, I don't have one school to show, which is actually doing something in terms of environmental conservation." Mr. Kumar names a number of reasons why this is the case. First of all, policy generation on environmental education happened with the National Curriculum Framework (NCF, 2005), yet the system is not ready, because the National Curriculum Framework for teachers, guiding them on how to implement the new policy on environmental education was set only in 2009 and implementation has not been mandatory. Moreover, under the National Curriculum Framework EE is not compulsory, it is only recommended to have EE infused in subjects. Using Mr. Kumar's words: "Infusion is confusion". EE is neglected to a large extent, because it is not compulsory, not a graded subject and there is no monitoring. In addition, Mr. Kumar refers to the intervention strategies undertaken by WWF and CEE. He appreciates their work and the role they have in the sphere, but mentions that WWF-India, is a fancy organisation working with the elite schools only (approximately 100 ICSE and CBSE schools), the only benefit being the media effect. With regard to CEE, he points out that lack of funding led to the discontinuation of their training programs, and their key area now is material development. Moreover, both organisations avoid dealing with the larger structures and build their programmes on the 'crippled' education system.

According to Mr. Kumar, to generate a true effect, one has to take a structural approach, which in this particular case means addressing the teacher system. The revised strategy, which is being implemented since 6 months now, does not aim at environmental awareness or environmental action, but at environmental discipline." Habits are required and habits should be formed". The approach is to have an authority figure at school, to whom the 'green soldiers' look up to and from whom they accept and follow commands (Mr. Kumar has found the physical education teacher to be such an authority figure. For details on the approach see appendix 3).

At this point in time it is too early to evaluate if this new strategy will have an effect. There is scepticism and resistance from the school's side, partly because this approach does not seem very democratic, but rather dictatorial. Yet, according to Mr. Kumar his approach is similar to the ones taken by democratic countries in this world, where laws and regulations govern people on how to behave environmentally correct.

3.4 External factors determining REB in secondary school children

Based on the presented findings external factors possibly facilitating or prohibiting the implementation of the 'Solar powered Schools in Hyderabad' project can be summed up as follows.

First, secondary education in India is institutionally diverse, which results in inhomogeneity of textbook content, teaching methods and consequently knowledge and development of children. Moreover the demographic background of children is quite discrepant between public and private schools.

Second, policies have been developed towards improving the school curriculum in terms of having a more activity based teaching system versus knowledge generation only, and infusing EE across all subjects. However, the necessary antecedent, which is a change in teacher training, is insufficient. In addition, the curriculum is overloaded and competition between schools in terms of final examination is high. Therefore, barriers could be lack of motivation and time by teachers. Working with state-governed schools is particularly challenging, since here the teaching approach is still learning by rote, control and monitoring over teachers is missing, and schools' resources are constrained.

On the positive side, there are a number of NGOs working with children in Hyderabad towards environmental awareness and conservation. They have many years of experience and are involved in a variety of activities depending on their strategy. CEE employs a constructivist approach aimed at awareness generation, mainly through teacher education and material design. The large pool of partnerships with other NGOs is beneficial. WWF, likewise, follows the cognitive approach to behaviour change towards REB in children. The Young Climate Savers programme, undertaken in a number of selected private schools, actively organises information based activities. Facilitating for WWF-India is the organisation's proliferation and long time experience, as well as their efficiency in using mass communication channels, which results in strong brand awareness.

In contrary to CEE and WWF, the director of NGC Andhra Pradesh has lately decided to implement a different strategy. Based on the psychological theory of behaviourism, this strategy aims to create habits in children en route to environmental conservation. The final goal envisaged is visibility of REB at school level. The NGC is well-established in Andhra Pradesh, reaching out to 5,750 schools and their previous strategy has raised awareness in children. Equal to CEE, NGC was established by the MoEF, Government of India, as such these organisations are in a strong position when intervention strategies aim to change public policy.

Finally, all three NGOs discussed are certainly opinion leaders in India's environmental movement, yet they face challenges due to financial, time and human resource constraints, as well as the discussed institutional barriers at school level.

After having identified the external factors which presumably affect environmental behaviour in children in Hyderabad, in the next chapter, the attention shifts to an analysis of internal factors.

4 Internal Factors determining behaviour

As mentioned in the methodology, in order to answer research question three: "What is the awareness and behaviour of children from secondary schools on environmental issues and low-emission lifestyles prior to project implementation?" a quantitative research approach was chosen.

The study employed a survey design in form of a paper-based, self reported questionnaire (Appendix 5).

4.1 Procedure and participants

A total of nine secondary schools were selected for the study through non-random purposive sampling (expert consultation). Having a number of schools from the different management boards was considered, as well as the fact that they had cooperated with environmental organisations before. Two schools were chosen, for the particular reason that they are assigned partners of the trial project. A total of 280 students from 9th and 10th standard (aged 14-16) participated in the study. The questionnaires were distributed and completed in the classroom, in the presence of the investigator and the teacher. This enabled the removal of potential misapprehensions deriving from the questions at hand or language barriers[9]. Out of the 280 distributed questionnaires, 200 were filled in without errors or missing data; consequently this value represents the sample size of this study.

4.2 Conceptual Model

The variables for the study were chosen so as to assess the children's knowledge, awareness, attitude (personality) and behaviour toward environmental issues and to understand the causal relationships among antecedents of responsible environmental behaviour. The underlying assumption is that people use information available to them in a reasonable manner to arrive at a decision on whether to act or not act environmentally friendly.

Of the alternative concepts presented in the literature review, Hines' et al. (1986 cited in Bamberg & Möser, 2007) Model of Responsible Environmental Behaviour (REB) seems most appropriate for this particular case.

The measured variables in this study reflect the components of the REB model, excluding situational factors, which have been discussed in the previous chapters. With reference to the objective of understanding to what extent children are aware of environmental issues, it is acknowledged that the model of REB encompasses 'knowledge' as an indicator. Yet the findings in the literature review concerning appraisal processes (Homburg & Stolberg, 2006; Story & Forsyth, 2008), gave reason to include one further affective factor, namely 'threat appraisal', emanating from the protection motivation theory (Rogers, 1975 cited in Maddux & Rogers, 1983), for the evaluation of awareness.

In Figure 4 the conceptual model underlying this quantitative study is presented.

4.3 Measures

Environmental knowledge is categorised into two levels: (a) *abstract knowledge,* which relates to conceptual knowledge about the issue and (b) *concrete knowledge,* referring to

---

[9] Note: Primary language of teaching for all participants was English.

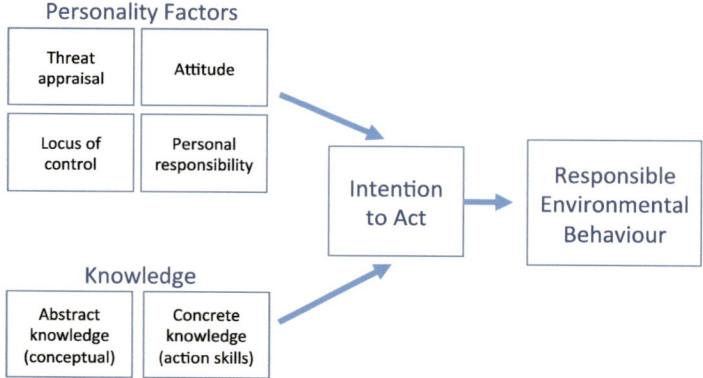

Figure 4: Conceptual model for study

Source: Based on Hines' *et al.* (1986, cited in Kollmuss & Agyeman, 2002) Model of Responsible Environmental Behaviour, extended by variable 'threat appraisal' adopted from Protection Motivation Theory [Rogers, 1983]

a person's understanding of environmental action and action skills. To measure *abstract knowledge* a set of thirteen questions addressing a range of topics including climate change and global warming, as well as energy, water, land and resource conservation was developed to understand if participants had heard about and could explain concrete issues. In addition, five true/false questions referred to abstract knowledge. Another five true/false questions were asked in regard to *concrete knowledge*, besides the task to name particular activities an individual can do to protect the environment. Up to a maximum of four open ended questions have been counted.

Four dimensions of *personality factors* were investigated, with one scale each for: attitude, locus of control, personal responsibility and threat appraisal. All scales contained two items; the response range for all items was a 5-point scale, ranging from 'strongly agree' to 'strongly disagree'.

Attitude describes an individual's favourable or unfavourable feelings with regard to particular issues. The questions in this study were phrased according to Hines *et al.* categorisation of attitude toward ecology and environment as a whole, and attitude toward taking action.

Locus of Control means an individual's belief in whether he or she has the ability to bring about change through his or her own behaviour. In the survey, one question referred to the perceived power of others (external locus of control), and another to the respondent's ability to act (internal locus of control).

Personal Responsibility is defined as a personal obligation or sense of duty to implement actions. In order to measure responsibility two items were used, one of them was: "Solving the problem is not my responsibility."

Threat appraisal refers to a person's perceived severity or harm stemming from a situation. It can also be referred to as environmental concern and involves the emotionality that an individual expresses in relation to ecological issues. In this study threat appraisal refers to the participant's belief about the degree to which the immediate environment is polluted and the concern about dangers deriving from pollution for personal wellbeing.

Intention to act is indicated by a person's subjective perspective and report of the probability that he or she will perform the behaviour in question. It can be understood as the stated willingness to act upon environmental problems. In this study, two questions related to intention to act, concerning one to the willingness to learn more about environmental issues and second willingness to change lifestyle.

As a further substitute for actual behaviour, reported *responsible environmental behaviour* (REB) has been measured, thereby, taking the limitation into consideration that it does not accurately reflect actual behaviour. Items on responsible environmental behaviour were related to energy, waste, water, natural resources, mode of transport, as well as advising others or being member of an eco-club or organisation.

In addition to the described variables, the instrument also prompted the respondents for demographic information such as gender, school name and school type; In respect to knowledge the questionnaire also contained an item on 'source of knowledge'.

To assist in interpreting the data, ranges for scale items were determined (See Table 2). For knowledge one point was assigned to each correct answer in the true/false questions, for 'having read/heard about an issue, as well as for the number of activities 'one can do to protect the environment' named.

The four personality factors and the item 'intended behaviour', consisted of two items each with a 5 point scale (2=strongly agree to -2=strongly disagree), leading to a range of -4 to 4 for each variable (0 for both items remained 0). For REB the respondents received one point if the answer was 'yes' to a range of questions on actions undertaken and one point if the explanation in question 11 in the questionnaire was given.

4.4 Data Analysis and Results

The first statistical operations aimed at generating descriptive statistics on the variables as measured on the respective scales, resulting in means and standard deviation. This

Table 2: Descriptive statistics and Cronbach's Alpha

Variable	Items	Range	M	SD	α
Y1: Abstract Knowledge	18	0 – 18	16.0	2.3	.92
Y2: Concrete Knowledge	7	0 – 7	6.1	1.6	.72
Y3: Attitude	2	-4 – 4	1.6	1.7	<.70
Y4: Locus of Control	2	-4 – 4	-1.0	1.7	<.70
Y5: Personal Responsibility	2	-4 – 4	1.0	1.8	<.70
Y6: Threat Appraisal	2	-4 – 4	2.6	1.4	<.70
Y7: Intended Behaviour	2	-4 – 4	2.4	1.2	<.70
Y8: REB	9	0 – 9	7.8	2.7	.71

was followed by calculation of Cronbach's alpha (α) to test for reliability. The results are summarised in Table 2.

The internal consistency of the scale 'abstract knowledge' was very satisfying, with $\alpha = .92$. After elimination of two true/false items from the 'concrete knowledge' scale, the Cronbach alpha was .72. The Cronbach alpha for all four personality factors and the factor 'intention to act' were below the acceptable value of .70, due to the fact that the value of alpha depends on the number of items on the scale, which here was only two items per scale. This is a limitation of the study, since an alpha below the .07 value is too low to generalise the measurement errors for the factors. However, Kline (1999 cited in Field, 2006) states that when handling psychological constructs values below .70, can, realistically, be assumed, due to the diversity of the constructs being measured. Consequently, these factors were nevertheless used in the conceptual model of the study.

Variance analysis across school type

Next, one-way analysis of variance (ANOVA) for the discrete variable school type (considered as most important amongst the discrete variables with respect to the overall study) with the dependent variables from the categories knowledge, personality factors and behaviour was undertaken, in order to determine if differences exist across group means and to analyse total means of the dependent variables.

In addition, simple comparison of means was carried out between the discrete variables 'source of knowledge' and 'school type' in order to determine the dominant source of respondent's knowledge, which is considered to have important implications for the study.

The results of the one-way analysis of variance, as shown in Figure 5[a, c, d], are all significant, since the significance value p is less than or equal to the standard alpha level of .05 in all cases. For abstract knowledge, concrete knowledge, attitude and threat appraisal, the p-value is .000, indicating that the odds of having a difference between the mean scores of school type to the mean scores of these variables due to random chance is less than 1 in 1,000. Moreover, the f-value, indicating fit of results is significantly higher than 1. For the factors personal responsibility, locus of control, behaviour intention an REB, the significance level was p<.05 and f was likewise larger than one.

- Students from government schools scored only 50 % in questions on concrete knowledge (below total mean of 80 %), and 70 % on abstract knowledge questions (below total mean of 90 %), while ICSE students answered on average 95 % of the knowledge questions correctly.

- All respondents have a somewhat positive attitude towards the environment, yet CBSE and ICSE student's scores for attitude are significantly higher.

- A sensed threat stemming from the effects of climate change and a fear of a decreased quality of environment due to pollution is common across the groups, however much lower for government students than ICSE students.

- Except for government students, the respondents from the other groups somewhat agree that they are personally responsible for solving environmental problems (total mean=1.0).

- The variable 'locus of control' has a negative total mean value, which indicates that respondents have low self-efficacy and strong external locus of control. Particularly students from government schools consider others as more powerful to act, and believe they lack skills to take action to improve the state of the environment.

- While knowledge as well as a positive attitude towards environment and a feeling of personal responsibility increase from government over SSC to CBSE and finally ICSE schools, the mean scores of intended behaviour and reported REB is somewhat equal across school types (Lower f-value and higher p-value for intended behaviour and REB, in comparison to the values for the other variables also indicate the difference in means for behaviour variables is not as significant as for the knowledge and personality factor variables). A total mean of 2.5 for intended behaviour is relatively high on the (-)4 to (4) point scale. Likewise, respondents answered 'yes' to more than half of the question relating to REB (total mean 5 out of 9).

Comparison of means between knowledge and source of knowledge for the four school types (Figure 5b) revealed that all respondents gained most of their abstract knowledge from school, followed by books. Media accounted for 42 % of knowledge. For the group government, parents and representatives of environmental NGOs visiting schools were non-accountable sources of knowledge, in contrast to the other school types. Overall NGOs generated the least knowledge. Interesting to note is that close peers (parents and friends together), constituted for 40 % of abstract knowledge.

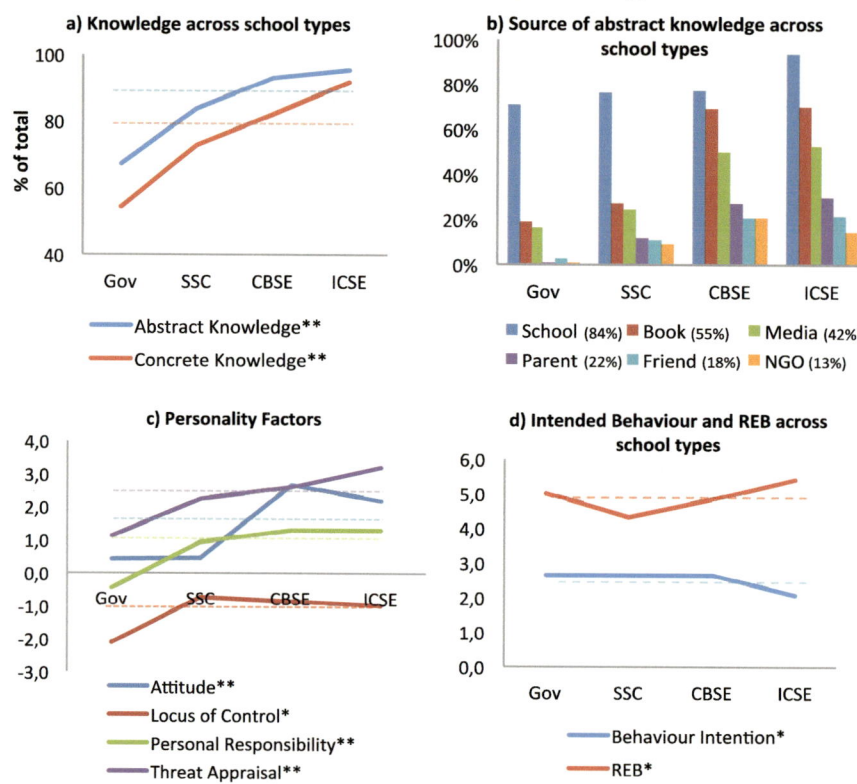

Figure 5: Variances across school types

(Note: Dotted lines in Figure [a, c, d] and %-values in legend of Figure [b] indicate mean for totals); ANOVA F-ratios: $F>15$ for Abstract Knowledge, Concrete Knowledge, Attitude and Threat Appraisal; $F>3$ for Personal Responsibility, Locus of Control, Behaviour Intention, REB. Significance values: **$p<.001$; *$p<.05$)

Having established the level of knowledge, personality factors and behaviour, the analysis went on to test the conceptual model underpinning the study and to investigate cause-effect relationships between variables.

Multiple Regression Analysis

The Multiple Regression Analysis was undertaken to determine which of the independent variables have the highest correlation[10] to REB. Therefore, a stepwise analysis was conducted.

First, 'intended behaviour' was entered *by force* as the independent variable to the dependent variable REB, based on the assumption adopted from Hines *et al.* (1986, cited in Bamberg & Möser, 2007) that it is a direct antecedent. This was followed by including the remaining independent variables (knowledge and personality factors) into the equation (method: stepwise).

The results of the multiple regression analysis used to test the conceptual model are summarised in Table 3. They indicate that behaviour intention, concrete knowledge and attitude predict REB. The other independent variables failed to meet the significance value of p<.05 and therefore have been excluded. In the first Step, where only behaviour intention was related to REB, the predictor accounts for only 7% (R^2) variance in the dependent variable. In Step 2 concrete knowledge was added to the equation, which led to an 11% increase in R^2. Finally, the third model, consisting of intended behaviour, concrete knowledge and attitude as predictors for REB, had the best fit ($R^2 = .21$).

For interpretation of results, the standardised beta values (β) and their significance are important statistics to look at, as they indicate the number of standard deviations (SD) that the dependent variable will change as a result of one SD change in the independent variable and give an idea of the 'importance' of a predictor in the model (Field, 2008).

In the third model (Step 3) all β are positive and highly significant. The standardised beta value for behaviour intention is .23**, for concrete knowledge .27** and for attitude .19**. Since all three coefficients lie below the value of .30 the strengths of the relations have only limited practical value. Besides, concrete knowledge has the highest impact in the model.

These results stand in contradiction to the suggestion of Hines *et al.* (1986, cited in Bamberg & Möser, 2007) that intended behaviour is strongly related to REB and that abstract knowledge, as well as personal responsibility and locus of control are important indirect predictors, along with attitude and concrete knowledge. In addition,

---

[10] Correlation coefficients can take values from -1 to 1. When r=0 there is no relation, otherwise the variables are either positively related (1), moving in the same direction, or negatively related (-1), while one variable increases the other decreases. A general guideline for the strengths of the relationship is (1) correlations below .30 are of little practical value (2) correlations in the range of .30 to .50 may be considered moderate magnitude and (3) a strong relationship is indicated by a correlation exceeding .50 (Ajzen & Fishbein, 1980).

Table 3: Multiple Regression Analysis

Independent Variables	b	SE b	B
Step 1			
Behaviour Intention	0.46	0.12	.27***
Step 2			
Behaviour Intention	0.44	0.11	.26***
Concrete Knowledge	0.43	0.08	.33***
Step 3			
Behaviour Intention	0.39	0.11	.23***
Concrete Knowledge	0.36	0.09	.27***
Attitude	0.23	0.08	.19**

Dependent Variable: REB
$R^2 = .07$ for Step 1, $\Delta R^2 = .11$ for Step 2, $\Delta R^2 = .143$ for Step 3;
*p<.05, **p<.01, ***p<.001

the hypothesis that threat appraisal will be associated with REB would have to be rejected according to these findings. It is assumed that the contradictions to outcomes of previous studies (Hines et al. 1986; Homburg & Stolberg, 2006; Story & Forsyth, 2008) are a result of insufficient reliability of measures of personality factors and intended behaviour in this study ($\alpha<.70$), which is clearly a limitation.

Leaving the strengths of relation aside, the multiple regression analysis, after all showed that there are statistically significant relations between REB and the independent variables concrete knowledge, attitude and intended behaviour.

However, it did not test for any relationships among the independent variables in the model and does not give any insights of relations between the excluded variables.

Therefore, the last statistical operation was a simple correlation of the dependent and independent scale variables to produce Pearson's correlation coefficient (r), as a means of describing the strengths of relationships among variables.

Pearson's product-moment correlation coefficients

A summary of results is provided in Table 4. Significant associations found between variables are described, as follows:

- The relationship between each of the independent variables: concrete knowledge, attitude and intended behaviour to REB are consistent with the results of the multiple regression analysis.

- Whereas the results for the tested model from the multiple regression analysis had little practical value ($\beta<.30$ for all three variables) the correlation coefficients for concrete knowledge and REB (.38**) as well as attitude and REB (.31**) are statistically and practically significant.

- When looking at the intended behaviour, apart from the relation to REB (.27**), no other correlation is significant. This again must be ascribed to the limitation of low internal consistency of the variable Intended behaviour ($\alpha<.70$).

- As expected there is a relatively strong relation between concrete knowledge and abstract knowledge (46**).

- Moreover, the findings suggest that there is a moderate positive correlation between both knowledge factors and attitude ($r=0.31**$ for each). This implies that an increase in knowledge is related to a stronger pro-environmental attitude.

- Significant is also the positive relationship between concrete knowledge and threat appraisal, which is moderate with $r=.35**$. Moreover, abstract knowledge and threat appraisal are relatively strongly related ($r=.44**$). This means in practical terms, a raised level of knowledge is associated with a higher belief in one's ability to cope with threat stemming from environmental pollution/destruction.

- Statistically significant, yet of little practical value are the correlations for attitude and threat appraisal (.29**), as well as personal responsibility (.23**). The latter is also significantly related to concrete knowledge (.26**) and locus of control (.29**).

Table 4: Pearson's product-moment correlation coefficient

Variable	Y1	Y2	Y3	Y4	Y5	Y6	Y7	Y8
Y1: Abstract Knowledge	1							
Y2: Concrete Knowledge	.46**	1						
Y3: Attitude	.31**	.31**	1					
Y4: Locus of Control	.17*	.10	-.02	1				
Y5: Personal Responsibility	.14*	.26**	.23**	.29**	1			
Y6: Threat Appraisal	.44**	.35**	.29**	.16*	.04	1		
Y7: Intended Behaviour	-.12	.03	.15*	.04	.26**	.05	1	
Y8: REB	.23**	.38**	.31**	.03	.19*	.20*	.27**	1

($n=200$; *$p<.05$, **$p<.001$)

Moving on to address the primary research question of the study, the results of the quantitative study will be discussed in conjunction with findings from the previous chapters.

5 Discussion

"Which factors facilitate or prohibit responsible environmental behaviour with regard to the 'Solar powered Schools for Hyderabad' project?" is the primary research question of this study. In relation to the question, the following objectives were set in the introduction:

1. Determination of theoretical background from literature on characteristics and strategy of the 'Solar powered Schools for Hyderabad' project

2. Identification of efforts undertaken by local actors to promote pro-environmental behaviour in children

3. Analysis of the level of knowledge, awareness and behaviour of children from secondary schools on environmental issues and low-emission lifestyles prior to project implementation

In order to derive an answer to the research question the objectives will be discussed in reverse order, starting with objective three. Implications for the pilot project at different levels (school, coalition building and community) will be discussed, as well as the overall project strategy based on theory.

Internal factors at school level

As evidence from the literature review has shown, it is a commonly accepted fact amongst academics that knowledge, attitude and behaviour are not related in a linear fashion. Ajzen & Fishbein (1980) in their TPB and Hines et al. (1986, cited in Bamberg & Möser, 2007) accordingly, suggest that intention to act is a direct antecedent of behaviour. In turn intended behaviour is determined by a number of variables.

The conceptual model applied in this case, which was based on Hines et al. (1986, cited in Bamberg & Möser, 2007) model of responsible environmental behaviour and extended by one further variable, namely threat appraisal, could not be confirmed, as the results of the multiple regression analysis have shown. At this point it should be stated that the aim of this qualitative study was not to test the model of REB, rather it was used in order to have a guideline for the decision on which variables to measure and analyse.

Since Cronbach's alpha of the variable 'intended behaviour' was below the acceptable value of .70 in this study and identification of relationships by calculating Pearson's correlation coefficient failed, no general conclusion can be drawn from results relating to this variable. Therefore, 'intended behaviour' will have to be factored out for the further discourse of this discussion. Instead, internal factors determining REB will be discussed by looking at the relationships between the remaining independent variables to reported REB.

The results of the multiple regression analysis as well as correlation coefficients suggest that there is a significant relationship between concrete knowledge and REB. It is important to note what the results suggest - only concrete knowledge directly determines REB, abstract knowledge however, does not. Hence, concrete knowledge is an important factor for the empowerment level, as proposed by Hines *et al.* (1986, cited in Bamberg & Möser, 2007). The findings furthermore showed that concrete knowledge is positively related to abstract knowledge, personal responsibility and threat appraisal, which implies that these factors indirectly influence REB, as confirmed by previous studies (Hines *et al.* 1986; Homburg & Stolberg, 2006; Story & Forsyth, 2008).

Therefore the first important implication for programmes aimed at behaviour change that can be drawn from these findings is that strategies should focus on generating concrete knowledge about environmental action, which means in practice communicating to the audience what can or in fact should be *done* in every day life to protect the environment. Thereby, abstract knowledge should be provided to the degree necessary in order for the individual to understand the reasoning behind the concrete knowledge. The transmitted information should moreover stress that every citizen has a responsibility to act.

Second, the variable threat appraisal, which resembles the level of concern for the environment, was included in the conceptual model, since many environmental intervention strategies aim at increasing awareness. The results suggest that threat appraisal, or in other words awareness about the environment, is related to concrete knowledge, and more importantly to abstract knowledge. However, no direct relationship between threat appraisal and REB was identified. Therefore, increased awareness alone does not lead to REB, which seems to be a common assumption amongst strategy designers. For intervention programmes this implies that the attention must not be put predominantly on generating abstract knowledge, which in turn will increase awareness, but on provision of concrete knowledge.

According to the findings the second variable directly related to REB is attitude. Ajzen & Fishbein (1980) consider attitude as one of the most important determinants of behaviour and other studies likewise confirm the significant relationship between these two factors (Hines *et al.* 1986; Wiseman & Bogner, 2003; Oerke 2007). Pearson's correlation coefficient analysis in chapter 4 showed that attitude in turn is related to the two knowledge factors, as well as personal responsibility and threat appraisal. Therefore, it can be assumed that the implication described in the previous paragraph will additionally have an influence on the audience's attitude. Theoretically, an increase in knowledge, resulting in more personal responsibility and higher concern for environment are also related to a more positive attitude towards taking protective and conservative action.

However, according to Petty and Cacioppo (1981 & 1986 cited in Petty, Briñol & Tormala, 2002) in practice attitude formation is dependent on the person's elaboration level. The suggested strategy will only work if the audience uses the central route of elaboration, where ideas are considered logically. On the other hand, if motivation is low and the issue is not of personal interest to the recipients, the peripheral route of elaboration might be dominating. In this scenario, contextual factors, such as attractiveness and credibility of source will influence the attitude formation.

The discussion will return to external factors and their implications for the pilot project, after deliberating on one further point in regard to internal factors.

As objective three states the aim of the statistical analysis was to identify the level of knowledge, attitude and behaviour of children, which holds important implications for the strategy design of the pilot project for the targeted schools. The 'Solar powered Schools for Hyderabad' project initially targets three secondary schools: two schools following the SSC board and one school complying with the ICSE board. Therefore, the variables have been examined across the different school types. It was found that knowledge, as well as attitude and personal responsibility increase from Government over SSC to CBSE and finally ICSE schools. Moreover, environmental awareness (threat appraisal) is considerably lower among government and SSC students, than in CBSE and ICSE students (Compare Figure 5).

Given the varying initial situations among the schools, it can be inferred that the pilot project needs different action plans for the school types. Based on the level of abstract knowledge, which is considered important in the entry level of behaving environmentally friendly (Hines et al. 1986), it can be assumed that ICSE students are more advanced than SSC students. While the implementation strategy for both school types should focus on generating concrete knowledge and changing attitudes through persuasive communication to empower the children, the spectrum of knowledge included in the information package might have to be broader for SSC students, than for ICSE students.

However, this implication will prove true only if we assume the children make reasoned choices. The earlier discussion suggested that children with higher conceptual knowledge and a more positive attitude would in turn show more responsible environmental behaviour. Yet the graphs shown in Figure 5 contradict this proposition.

For example, when looking at the group 'government schools', it can be seen that students scored far below average in terms of knowledge, attitude, threat appraisal and personal responsibility, yet their reported behaviour is equal to the mean, which is inconsistent with the hypothesis.

There can be a number of reasons why the results diverge from theory. First, insufficient reliability or validity of measures might be the cause; second, it might be due to a social desirability response bias, a common phenomenon in research employing self-reports. Respondents might have provided socially desirable answers, thereby over-reporting good behaviour or under-reporting bad behaviour, thus as a consequence the reported behaviour does not accurately reflect actual behaviour (Mortel, 2008). The third argument, which was elaborated in the literature review, is that external factors strongly influence responsible environmental behaviour, potentially even more than internal factors.

<u>External factors at school level</u>
From the learning theory (Skinner 1957, cited in Mills, 1998) we know that situational factors somehow control an individual's behaviour and that actions can be changed by variation of circumstances in which the behaviour occurs. The terms can be modified by provision of examples that can be imitated as a factor preceding behaviour or by installing rewards and punishments following the behaviour.

In the school environment, teachers undoubtedly set examples for children. Without intending to over-generalise, the extent to which teachers in secondary education in India can serve as role models in terms of environmentally friendly behaviour under the current education system is -regarding this particular issue- somewhat questionable.

On the positive side, the 'Solar powered Schools for Hyderabad' project team has already identified three schools that are keen on participating, which means that the principals have a vision and ambitions for change. Yet, a whole-school approach is necessary in order for the solar panel to be fully self-managed by the school. Therefore, the principal needs the skills and ability to motivate and evoke action in teachers, who are the connecting point to the students. The general conditions, however, differ across the school types.

The findings in Chapter 3 indicate that teachers working according to the SSC school system and curriculum do not have a good starting point to engage children in activities promoting environmental responsibility and in fact, the current situation might rather prohibit such efforts. For one, teachers are not sufficiently equipped with the necessary knowledge and skills to successfully bring about behaviour change in regard to environmental protection in children, due to the teacher's education. Moreover, the Indian education system is burdened by curriculum overload, high competition between schools in regard to examination results and teacher's assessment is deficient. In addition, the teaching method practiced in schools complying with the SSC board is concentrating on learning by rote, using outdated textbooks and assessment throughout the year by marking and grading. This implies that teachers might lack skills, time and motivation to bring up the extra effort imperative for encouragement of environmental behaviour in their students. The findings furthermore suggest that there is a danger of teachers not being accountable to principals, which puts a strain on the role of the headmaster as an effectual leader for change.

On the contrary, ICSE schools are in a better position for change, since they employ a forward-looking education approach, including a focus on practical learning, the all-round development of children, up-to-date textbooks and extra curricula activities. This is achieved by targeting the wealthier segments of the population, who can afford the high tuition fees. Moreover, in the private sector teachers receive the highest salaries at ICSE schools, which has a positive effect on their motivation and also their accountability to the headmaster and parents (Compare Appendix 1).

According to the mantra of communication theory 'who says what to whom with what effect' and based on the objectives of the pilot project at school level, which are self-management of solar panel, incorporation of the topic in curriculum, generation of knowledge, formation of attitude to an extent where the school is in a position to communicate the benefits of the innovation to the community and careful impact assessment, the following suggestions can be made for the strategy design:

- The goals, objectives and the concrete action plan, including the implied changes that will happen at the school as well as everyone's responsibilities and concrete tasks will have to be communicated to headmasters, teachers and students alike. A source for message dissemination could be the project team providing the information to the headmaster, who in turn will transfer it to teachers and students. Though, if feasible, direct communication from the project team to all stakeholders at the school might yield higher motivation and increased personal interest from the audience, since the message is delivered by an outside source, with expertise in the field.

- For generation of major concrete knowledge, and to some extent abstract knowledge on the solar panel, covering aspects such as the relative advantage of the innovation, its compatibility and complexity, experts will have to be appointed who can train teachers and headmasters.

- Subsequently, students will be educated by teachers, provided that sufficient time and space is allocated in the curriculum and content is agreed upon. This might be more challenging to achieve in SSC schools than in ICSE schools. Ideally, the initial persuasive communication by the project team and experts to teachers and headmasters is effective enough for them to act on their own authority. However, the strategic plan should include components of evaluation and control. Human and financial assistance will probably be required for content and material design.

- To increase motivation and ensure efficient documentation of impacts, incentives will have to be installed. For example, inter-school or cross-school competitions could be established pertaining to the amount of energy saved, ideas for utilization of surplus energy or efforts undertaken by schools to disseminate the innovation in the community, including rewards following successful behaviour.

To achieve these objectives, financial and human resources will be required. Given that the project team is not permanently staying in India, partnerships will have to be built for the implementation of the project. In Chapter 3 a range of players and their strategies have been presented and opportunities deriving from possible partnerships will be discussed in the following.

Opportunities by means of partnerships
Cooperating with Yardstick for the pilot project holds a number of opportunities. First, they have know-how in working with schools towards making learning a joyful and enriching experience and are aware of the local conditions. Moreover, the employees have an entrepreneurial mindset and have a background in engineering and teaching,

which enables them to create material and low-cost scientific models that are employed for hands-on learning. Solar panel related material and models could be developed that will help children and teachers in learning the complex scientific theory behind the innovation. Rebuilding simple models of the solar panel in class, which the children can take home, would moreover help in disseminating the innovation in the community.

The findings in regard to CEE suggest that the organisation is very experienced in the field of child-friendly material design on environmental issues. A content analysis of existing sources on the topic of solar energy and low emission lifestyles is recommended. Likewise, their expertise will be valuable for development of new matter. Currently, CEE is not targeting schools in urban Hyderabad; however, they have cooperated with a range of NGOs in the past in this regard, which might hold unexplored opportunities for partnerships. Moreover, CEE has a direct connection to the Ministry of Environment and Forest, the Government of India, which is a valuable position for interventions aiming at policy change.

The latter also applies to NGC, which is working with 5,750 schools in the greater Hyderabad region. A partnership could provide access to these sources, which would be beneficial for the up-scaling of the project. While the recently revised strategy of NGC is not up for discussion, it has given a thought-provoking impulse. One idea is that change should be visible, which will be achieved in the pilot project by installing the solar panel. Second, it became evident that the physical education teacher, who for example manages the assembly in the morning, holds a special position in the school. It is envisaged that the technical equipment provided for the schools includes a child-friendly instrument for measuring the energy generated and used which will be installed in a central place in the school. Therefore, it should be considered if a system whereby the energy is measured by children can be included in the morning assembly routine headed by the physical education teacher.

Finally, a coalition with WWF-India might act as a good media-magnet, since they are the country's largest and oldest nature-conservation organisation and have established high brand awareness in India. As such, attractiveness of source for local print and TV agents could increase by working with WWF-India. Moreover, in terms of electronic messaging, a link to WWF-India's web-portals could help in increasing outreach.

In general, cooperating with Yardstick or CEE as discussed earlier will require incentives for the partners, since both organisations are constrained in terms of financial and human resources. That said, the project's budget presumably does not allow for major monetary rewards, which is a disadvantage for the building of the proposed coalitions.

One possible incentive might be publicity. The literature review as well as the findings in Chapter 4 suggest that media is an important source of information on aspects relating to climate change. This also has important implications for message dissemination at the community level. Therefore, generating media interest should be an important element of the pilot project's strategy.

After having discussed factors that have an impact on the short term aims of the 'Solar powered Schools for Hyderabad' project, in the following paragraph the overall strategy and particularly the mid-and long-term aims will be discussed in regard to the generated findings and what was learned from the literature review.

Evaluation of strategic approach

The literature review revealed that the application of interventions aimed at changing certain behaviour is preceded by the thorough selection of behaviours to be changed and an analysis of causes of those behaviours (Geller, 2002; cited in Steg & Vlek, 2008).

As presented in Chapter 2, extensive research and effort was invested in the 2-year long pre-phase of the 'Sustainable Hyderabad' programme, to identify issues that need to be addressed to enhance environmental quality in Hyderabad as well as causes of those problems, which ultimately led to the decision to develop a pilot project dealing with alternative energy at school level.

The project aims have been set to achieve outcomes across a number of sectors. An individual behaviour change campaign at school level towards raised awareness and change in lifestyle by installation of solar panels intends to generate important evidence that can be employed for dissemination of the innovation at community level and initiation of policy change in regard to alternative energy, which is the ultimate goal.

As such the programme tries to create a chain reaction from individual behaviour change to public will generation to eventually achieve policy change. According to Coffman (2003) the characteristic of using individual change and a public will component in conjunction for bringing about change in policy has been found only recently in campaigns towards change. And in fact, research suggests that this is the way forward. Only through decentralised planning and implementation of programmes by including the grassroots population and considering the socio-cultural context will development projects towards sustainability be successful.

Implementing the pilot project at schools is a good strategic approach. If the implementation at school level is successful, taking the facilitators and barriers discussed earlier into consideration for the development of the concrete action plan, the students and teachers can act as opinion leaders within their community. The school will be in a position to persuading the community of the relative advantage, compatibility and complexity of using alternative energy. Moreover, reporting and communicating the results of the project and achieved benefits for the schools will show trial-ability of the innovation with visible results.

Besides using interpersonal channels as a means for communicating the idea, mass media is a commonly employed tool for message dissemination. For the social diffusion of the idea within the community persuasive communication through media is applied and agenda setting serves the advancement of policy change, as suggested by Coffman (2003).

In terms of agenda setting the 'Jawaharlal Nehru National Solar Mission', which has been declared by the Indian government (Compare Chapter 2), has generated large media interest, which seems an ideal situation for the 'Solar powered School for Hyderabad' project to establish a foothold. Moreover, with regard to persuasive communication through media the project team has considered the use of new media and social networks as tools for PR. The move in Hyderabad towards a modern consumer society implicates an increase in the use of the internet. However, this trend has been registered only within the middle and higher classes of the population. For the majority of the population traditional media, like print, TV and radio, still constitutes the main source of information (Datamonitor, 2010). Therefore, it is highly recommended to elaborate in greater detail the use of media as a communication tool.

Overall, the strategy's characteristics can be summed up as 'change must be broad in order to be deep'. The achievement of the mid- and long-term goals will be fully dependent on the success of the pilot project at school level.

The installation of solar panels in the school is a major structural change, which is seen as an important determining factor towards responsible environmental behaviour change. Additional contextual and internal factors will influence the success of the project, which the previous discussion has attempted to put some light upon, and ideally will be considered for the design of the implementation strategy of the 'Solar powered Schools for Hyderabad' project.

Contribution from literature and limitations

As stated in the introduction, a further implication of the study was to derive at a conclusion to what extent current knowledge from literature and academics enables examination of environmental behaviour antecedents and how this knowledge helps in establishing a guideline for the strategy design in regard to a particular case, as well as what limitations exist.

With regard to the applied methodology, the conducted secondary research and interviews provided detailed information on education and NGOs actively working towards increased awareness and behaviour change on environmental issues. Moreover, it helped in designing the questionnaire. While qualitative research might have provided better insight into beliefs and behaviours of children on the topic, the quantitative study proved to be useful in studying the relationships between variables and helped form conclusions about the level of knowledge, attitude and practice of this particular sample of the population being studied, in a way that a general social trend could be identified. The research is, however, limited in terms of reliability of measures, which is due to the limited number of items on some measurement scales. Yet, extending the questionnaire by further items to improve reliability of scales would have been disadvantageous, taking the probable decrease in children's motivation to answer an even longer set of questions into consideration.

Given that evaluation research is vast and requires different research methodologies depending on the case under discussion, it is felt that the degree of freedom taken in regard to chosen methods and applied theory in this study is acceptable.

The literature review helped in identifying established knowledge on the topic; especially the field of theories on human behaviour and internal factors determining behaviour change is extensive. However, no general rules of thumb or overarching concepts have been agreed upon as of yet by researches and a number of concepts and hypothesis coexist. As such, researchers draw from the large pool of knowledge, constructing their own concepts, yielding an even greater dispersion.

Moreover, in terms of external factors influencing responsible environmental behaviour, the availability of sound findings and guidelines for application to practical cases and strategy design is scarce. Nevertheless, past research cannot be underestimated; in fact academics have made important contributions, which have substantially helped in bringing this study forward.

6 Conclusion

The previous discussion constituted a formative evaluation of determining factors for responsible environmental behaviour prior to implementation of the 'Solar powered Schools in Hyderabad' project.

The growth of Hyderabad into a megacity brings economic and social development, but at the same time stresses city attributes such as living space, transport, resource allocation and the ecological system. With citizens' change in lifestyle, private, commercial and indirect energy use increase, this worsens problems of pollution and natural resource exploitation and fosters the climate change effect. To ensure long-term economic growth in the region, strategies for a sustainable development and addressing the arising problems, need to be developed. As presented in Chapter 2 of this study, one particular project, currently being planned as part of the 8-year programme 'Sustainable Hyderabad', deals with alternative energy at school level, to improve the school's energy supply and as such learning conditions, while at the same time fostering awareness of alternative energies and low emission lifestyles. The long term aim is policy change and the diffusion of innovations regarding alternative energies within the community with the ultimate outcome of an improved ecological situation in Hyderabad.

A review of existing theories on promotion of responsible environmental behaviour has shown that interventions aimed at changing cognitive factors (knowledge) and affective factors (feelings and emotions towards the subject), but more importantly structural factors are needed to effectively engage people in eco-friendly behaviour.

Concluding from these findings, it can be said that the strategy of the pilot project is well designed. The installation of solar panels in the schools is a major structural change for the three target schools. However, there are a number of hindering factors that need to be considered for the successful realisation of the project.

The analysis of characteristics of Indian secondary schools revealed that the school system is institutionally diverse and that, depending on the board the schools are affiliated to, different conditions prevail. The quality and standards of teaching, materials and student's development is significantly lower in SSC schools and government schools than schools complying with the CBSE and ICSE boards. Particular problems are a lack of evaluations and control of teachers, combined with the overloaded curriculum and high competition between schools in terms of final exam results. This leads to time constraints and low motivation, especially for teachers in government and SSC schools. ICSE and CBSE schools have a more modern teaching approach including for example, activity based learning and a better infusion of environmental education into the curriculum. A pilot project aimed at self-managed infusion of a new topic into the existing curriculum and teaching at the school therefore needs thorough pre-planning and provision of assistance, especially for the SSC schools in the target group. Moreover, evaluation and control measures are required, including rewards or even sanctions for an effective execution and the production of useful results of the project.

In Chapter 4 internal factors determining behaviour change have been examined, based on a conceptual framework developed from current theories. The most important finding is that the factors 'concrete knowledge' as well as 'attitude' are related to behaviour. Variables that were found to stand in relationship to these two major factors in turn are abstract knowledge, personal responsibility and threat appraisal. These theoretical findings imply that informative communication aimed at changing individual behaviour needs to concentrate on generating concrete knowledge about what needs to be done. The provision of abstract knowledge does have an influence on a person's threat appraisal, and increases awareness; however, this is not directly related to a change in behaviour. In regard to attitude formation, it was found that increased concrete knowledge also affects attitude, yet this will be dependent on a person's elaboration level. In practice, a source portraying high credibility and attractiveness in providing the message and generating motivation and interest in the audience will be majorly important in the persuasion process. A further significant finding is that the level of knowledge, personal responsibility, threat appraisal and attitude differed across the four school types, yet the reported behaviour did not show the same discrepancy. While this could be due to measurement flaws, it is argued that it is rather an indication of the limited value of informative interventions, commonly applied in communication strategies towards changing environmental behaviour and it highlights the importance of contextual factors influencing individual behaviour change.

This implies that the strategy for implementation at school level has to include the design of innovative activities away from the regular school routine in a way that students and teachers internalize the relative advantage, compatibility and degree of complexity of the innovation and in turn are enabled to be opinion leaders within their community so as to disseminate the idea.

To achieve this, coalitions with local partners will be required. Partnering with Yardstick might be a good opportunity in order to design out of the box, hands-on learning material in regard to the solar panel. Cooperating with CEE would likewise be useful for material design. Establishing synergies with WWF-India could have a positive impact on media interest. Negotiating talks might however be challenging since all organisations are constrained in terms of financial and human resources.

Overall, working with media for message dissemination will be important, since it is for one a motivating factor for the schools to utilise the installation to the best extent and second, it will have a great influence on spreading the word in the community. Concerning media activities, it is felt that the strategy of the pilot project has room for improvement.

The systematic front-end evaluation of contextual factors and internal factors in regard to the target group has disclosed critical aspects, which are recommended to be taken into consideration in the design of the strategy for the pilot project. Moreover, the generated knowledge can be built upon for the evaluation of process, outcome and impact after implementation.

In conclusion it can be said that the project team is taking a noble approach by providing solar panels for the schools. Preferably, this activity resembles a great structural change for the schools and already in itself is beneficial in the process of overcoming some of the institutional hurdles existent at schools and individual's internal factors that might hinder successful change. However, large efforts will be required by all stakeholders in achieving the objectives of the project and creating the desired effect from changing individual behaviour at school level to generating public will to live a sustainable lifestyle en route to assisting Hyderabad in the process of a sustainable development.

References

Abram, A., 1989. *Behaviorism, neobehaviorism, and cognitivism in learning therapy: historical and contemporary perspectives.* Hove : Lawrence Erlbaum Associates, 1989.

Ajzen, I. & Fishbein, M., 1980. *Understanding Attitudes and predicting social behaviour.* London: Prentice-Hall, 1980.

Babbie, E., 2007. *Research Methods in Sociology.* New Delhi, India: Wads-Worth, A Division of Cengage Learning.

Bales, S.N. & Gilliam, Jr, F.D., 2004. *Communications for Social Good.* Practice Matters – The Improving Philanthropy Project. New York: The Foundation Center. 2006. http://foundationcenter.org/gainknowledge/research/pdf/practicematters_08_paper.pdf [25-09-10].

Bamberg, S. & Möser, G., 2006. Twenty years after Hines, Hungerford, and Tomera: A new meta-analysis of psycho-social determinants of pro-environmental behaviour. *Journal of Environmental Psychology.* 2007, 27(1): 14–25.

BVIEER, 2002. *Study of Status of infusion of environmental concepts in school curricula and the effectiveness of its delivery.* Bharati Vidyapeeth Institute of Environment Education and Research (BVIEER). http://environment.bharatividya peeth.edu/html/Study%20of%20status.pdf [05-06-10].

BMBF, 2005-2010. Future Megacities. Megastädte von Morgen. Bundesministerium für Bildung und Forschung, Deutschland, (Federal Ministry of Education and Research, Germany.). 2005-2010. www.emerging-megacities.org/seiten-kopf/startseite/startseite-en.aspx [23-04-10].

Bogner, F.X., 2010. *Quantitative Methods in Environmental Education & Examples of Best Practice.* Conference Paper. 'Education and Climate Protection', Erkner, Germany, UFU, 2010.

Bördlein, C., 2009. *Eine Einführung in die Verhaltensanalyse (An introduction to behaviour analysis).* Christoph Bördlein: verhalten.org, 2009. http://verhalten.org/dateien/verhaltenbuch.pdf [04-10-10].

Brown, P., Chaskin, R.J., Hamilton, R. &Richman, H., 2003. *Toward Greater Effectiveness in Community Change: Challenges and Responses for Philanthropy.* Practice Matters – The Improving Philanthropy Project. New York: The Foundation Center. 2006. http://foundationcenter.org/gainknowledge/research/pdf/practicematters_03_paper.pdf [25-09-10].

CEE, 2010. Centre for Environment Education [Homepage], CEE Andhra Pradesh. www.ceeindia.org/cee/andhra.html [20-05-10].

Chetan, V., 2009. *Urban Issues, Reforms and Way Forward in India.* Department of Economic Affairs, Ministry of Finance, Government of India, July 2009. Working Paper No.4/2009 –DEA.

Coffman, J., 2003. *Lessons in evaluating communication campaigns: Five case studies.* Cambridge, MA: Harvard Family Research Project. Prepared for the Communications Consortium Media Center, Washington DC, 2003. www.mediaevaluation project.org/HFRP2.pdf [12-09-10].

Coffman, J., 2002. *Public Communication Campaign Evaluation: An Environmental Scan of Challenges, Criticism, Practice, and Opportunities.* Cambridge, MA: Harvard Family Research Project. Prepared for the Communications Consortium Media Center, Washington DC, 2002. www.mediaevaluationproject.org/HFRP. pdf [12-09-10].

Cottrell, S.P. & Graefe, A.R., 1997. Testing a conceptual framework of responsible environmental behaviour. *Journal of Environmental Education.* 1997, 29(1): 17–28.

Datamonitor, 2010. Industry Profile: Media in India. *Datamonitor,* September 2010. www.datamonitor.com [15-10-10].

Desai, V./ Potter, R.B. ed., 2006. *Doing Development Research.* New Delhi, India: Vistaar Publications, A Division of SAGE Publications India Pvt Ltd.

Field, A., 2006. Reliability Analysis. Online Handout as abridge version of Chapter 15 of Field, A., (2005) *Discovering Statistics using SPSS.* 2nd ed. London: Sage. www.statisticshell.com/reliability.pdf [05-08-10].

Field, A., 2008. Multiple Regression. Online Handout as abridge version of Chapter 7 of Field, A., (2009) *Discovering Statistics using SPSS: and sex and drugs and rock 'n' roll.* 3rd ed. London: Sage. www.statisticshell.com/multireg.pdf [05-08-10].

Frontiers, 2005. *Going for Grip Parity.* BP Global, Reports and Publications – Frontiers, Issue 12, 2005. www.bp.com/genericarticle.do?categoryId=9013609&contentId= 7005395 [12-10-10].

Ghosh, A., 2006. Communication Technology and Human Development, Recent Experiences in the Indian social sector. New Delhi, India: SAGE Publications India Pvt Ltd.

Geertz, C., 1973. Thick Description: Toward an Interpretive Theory of Culture, Chapter 1. Available from Anglia Ruskin University, Module BC 415009S, Managing Across Cultures, 2009/2010.

Gillham, B. 2007. *Research Interview: A range of techniques.* Maidenhead: Open University Press.

Griffin, E., 2006. *A first look at communication theory*. 6th ed. New York: McGraw-Hill.

Hagedorn, K., 2006. *Welcome to the website of the Megacity Project Hyderabad!* Sustainable Hyderabad Website. Division of resource economics, Humboldt University Berlin. 2006. www.sustainable-hyderabad.de/index.php?page=home [10-05-10].

Harriss-White, B., Rohra, S. & Singh, N., 2009. Political Architecture of India's Technology System for Solar Energy. *Economic & Political Weekly*. [Special Articles], 44/47, Nov 2009.

Hwang, Y-H., Kim, S-I. & Jeng, J-M., 2000. Examining the Causal Relationships Among Selected Antecedents of Responsible Environmental Behaviour. *The Journal of Environmental Education*. 2000. 31(4): 19–25.

Joshi, M., 2005. *ESD in India: Current practices and Development Plans*. Centre for Environment Education. Green Teacher!, Paper 22, Sept 2005. http://greenteacher.org/?page_id=47 [15-05-10].

Kaiser, F.G., Oerke, B. & Bogner, F.X., 2007. Behaviour-based environmental attitude: Development of an instrument for adolescents. *Journal of Environmental Psychology*. 2007, 27(3): 242–251.

Kollmuss, A. & Agyeman, J., (2002). Mind the Gap: why do people act environmentally and what are the barriers to pro-environmental behavior? *Environmental Education Research*. 2002, 8(3): 239–260.

Langdridge, D., Sheeran, P., Connolly, K.J., 2007. Analyzing Additional Variables in the Theory of Reasoned Action. *Journal of Applied Social Psychology*. 2007, 37(8): 1884–1913.

Maddux, J.E. & Rogers, R.W., 1983. Protection motivation and self-efficacy: A revised theory of fear appeals and attitude change. *Journal of Experimental Social Psychology*. 1983, 19(5): 469–479.

McQuail, D., 2010. *McQuail's Mass Communication Theory*. 6th ed. London: Sage Publications Ltd.

Mills, J.A., 1998. *Control [electronic source]: A History of Behavioural Psychology*, E-Book, New York University Press 1998.

MoEF, 2010a. *Annual Report 2009-10*. Ministry of Environment and Forests, Government of India, 2010. http://moef.gov.in/report/report.html [17-10-10].

MoEF, 2010b. *Report to the People on Environment and Forests 2009-2010*. Ministry of Environment and Forests, Government of India, 2010. http://moef.nic.in/downloads/public-information/Report%20to%20the%20People.pdf [17-10-10].

Moemeka, A.A., 1997. Development Communication for Developing Societies: Facing the Realities. *International Communication Gazette.* 1997, 59(4): 379–393.

Mortel, T.F. van de, 2008. Faking it: social desirability response bias in self-report research. *Australian Journal of Advanced Nursing.* 2008, 25(4): 40–48.

nexus, 2010a. *Participative Energy Management – socio technical experiments for low emission lifestyles.* Sustainable Hyderabad, WP6, paper 1B, Status Report, 08/2010. [Project internal paper].

nexus, 2010b. *Solar powered schools for Hyderabad.* Sustainable Hyderabad, WP6, Pilot Project Proposal, 07/2010. [Project internal paper]

Nikkha, H.A. & Redzuan, M.B., 2010. The Role of NGOs in Promoting Empowerment for Sustainable Community Development. *Journal of Human Ecology.* 30(2): 85–92.

Oerke, B., 2007. *Natur- und Umweltschutzbewusstsein: Dimensionalität und Validität beim Messen von Einstellungen und Verhalten (Nature- and environmental protection awareness: dimensionality and validity in measuring attitude and behavior).* Doctorial Thesis (Dr. rer. nat), Didactives of Biology, University of Bayreuth. http://deposit.d-nb.de/cgi-bin/dokserv?idn=988143674&dok_var=d1&dok_ext=pdf&filename=988143674.pdf [07-09-10].

Ohtomo, S. & Hirose, Y., 2007. The dual-process of reactive and intentional decision making involved in eco-friendly behaviour. *Journal of Environmental Psychology.* 2007, 27(2): 117–125.

Olson, J.M., 1993. Review: Everything You Always Wanted to Know about Attitudes. *Psychological Inquiry.* 1993, 4(4): 358–365.

Pelto, P.J. & Pelto, G.H., 1997. Studying Knowledge, Culture, and Behaviour in applied Medical Anthropology. *Medical Anthropology Quarterly.* 11(2): 147–163.

Petty, R.E., Briñol, P. & Tormala, Z.L., 2002. Thought Confidence as a Determinant of Persuasion: The Self-validation Hypothesis. *Journal of Personality and Social Psychology.* 2002, 82(5): 722–741.

Ravindranath, M.J., 2007. Environmental education in teacher education in India: experiences and challenges in the United Nation's Decade of Education for Sustainable Development. *Journal of Education for Teaching.* 33(2): 191–206.

Roberts, N.S., 2009. Impacts of the National Green Corps Program (Eco-Clubs) on students in India and their participation in environmental education activities. *Environmental Education Research.* August 2009, 15(4): 443–464.

Rodrigues, T.E.G., 2007. *A communication approach to responsible public environmental behaviour*. Conference Paper, Griffith University, Brisbane, Australia, 2007. www.tasa.org.au/conferences/conferencepapers07/papers/269.pdf [22-09-10].

Rogers, E.M., 1995. *Diffusion of Innovations*. 4th ed. New York, USA: The Free Press, A Division of Macmillan. Inc.

Sarabhai, K.V., approx. 2005. *EE and ESD – Good Practices and Challenges: A case study of India and CEE*. Centre for Environment Education. Green Teacher!, Paper 20. http://greenteacher.org/?page_id=47 [15-05-10].

Sarantakos, S., 2005. *Social Research*. 3rd ed. New York, USA: Palgrave Macmillan.

Shet, S., 2003. *Environmental Education finally finds a place in India's school textbooks*. InfoChange News & Features, Aug 2003. http://infochangeindia.org/20030804258/Education/Features/Environmental-education-finally-finds-a-place-in-India-s-school-textbooks.html [05-05-10].

Spreitzhofer, G., ca. 2006. *Megacities: Zwischen (Sub)urbanisierung und Globalisierung. (Megacities: Between (Sub)urbanization and globalization)*. Friedrich Ebert Stiftung, Online Akademie. http://library.fes.de/pdf-files/akademie/online/50340.pdf [20-04-10].

Srivastava, R., 2004. Test of boards: ICSE scores over SSC, CBSE. The Times of India, Feb/2004. Bennett, Coleman & Co. Ltd. http://timesofindia.indiatimes.com/city/mumbai/Test-of-boards-ICSE-scores-over-SSC-CBSE-/articleshow/520196.cms [15-06-10].

Steg, L. & Vlek, C., 2008. Encouraging pro-environmental behaviour: An integrative review and research agenda. *Journal of Environmental Psychology*. 2009, 29(3): 309–317.

TravelSmart Victoria, 2010. *Theories and Models of Behaviour Change*. Conducted by consultants for the Workplace and Education components of the TravelSmart program. Australia: Victorian Government and agency 'Sustainability Victoria', 2010. http://municipal.resourcesmart.vic.gov.au/resources/travelsmart---theories-and-models-of-behaviour-change.aspx [25-09-10].

Weidenboerner, K., 2008. Correlation of Affect, Verbal Commitment, Knowledge, Locus of Control and Attitude to Environmentally Responsible Behaviour in Designers of the Built Environment: Is Knowledge Enough? *The Forum on Public Policy*. 2008. www.forumonpublicpolicy.com/summer08papers/archivesummer08/Weidenboerner.pdf [13-10-10].

White, B., 2002. *Writing your MBA dissertation*. London, New York: Continuum.

World Bank, 2003. *Secondary Education in India.* South Asia Human Development Sector. Report No 2, 37833, Nov 2003. www-wds.worldbank.org/external/default/WDSContentServer/WDSP/IB/2006/10/27/000310607_20061027143638/Rendered/PDF/378330PAPER0SA1y0Education01PUBLIC1.pdf [07-08-10].

World Bank, 2009a. *Data – India.* The World Bank Group, 2010. http://data.worldbank.org/country/india [11-10-10].

World Bank, 2009b. *Secondary Education in India: Universalizing Opportunity.* South Asia Human Development Sector. Report No 2, 48521, Jan 2009. http://www-wds.worldbank.org/external/default/WDSContentServer/WDSP/IB/2009/05/18/000333037_20090518003954/Rendered/PDF/485210v20SR0wh10Box338913B01PUBLIC1.pdf [07-08-10].

WWF-India, 2010a. *Environment Education Program.* World Wide Fund for Nature – India. What we do – enablers – education. [Homepage]. www.wwfindia.org/about_wwf/enablers/education/ [14-08-10].

-India, 2010b. *Teacher's guide on climate change and energy.* World Wide Fund for Nature- India. Publications. 2010. http://assets.wwfindia.org/downloads/teacher_s_guide_on_climate_change___energy.pdf [14-08-10].

WWF-India, 2010c. World Wide Fund for Nature – India. [Homepage]. www.wwfindia.org [14-08-10].

Appendix

A.1 Interview – De Paul Kannamthanam (Yardstick)

Namaste! My name is Jenny Haberer from ARU Cambridge/MICA, Ahmedabad and I am working for the Indo-German Megacity project 'Sustainable Hyderabad', which is funded by the BMBF (Federal Ministry of Education and Research) and conducted in close cooperation with the Indian government.

My research aim is to understand the current knowledge, attitude and practice of school children and teachers in secondary education in Hyderabad about environmental issues and low-emission life-styles.

Therefore, I would also like to get an insight into extra-curriculum activities done by different agents and am thankful you're sharing your valuable time with me to learn about your organisation.

Name of organisation YARDSTICK
Name of Interviewee De Paul Kannamthanam
Date: 18/Jun/2010   Time: 15:00-16:00   Place: Yardstick Office, Sainikpuri, Hyderabad

The interview aims at getting insights into the following areas

Introduction

- Please tell me about your organisation in general. What is your vision/aim?
- What is your strategy, how do you address/ reach your target audience?
- Action Plan How do you go about achieving your vision (where when who what how)?

Insights

- What is the response?
- What are your biggest challenges, what barriers do you face?
- What are the facilitators?

Working with teachers, teacher's perspective:

- How is it to be a teacher in India, current attitudes, practices? (training, income, motivation)
- What feedback do you get on your practice/mission, response from teachers?
- What are the biggest problems?

Future

- What must change for teachers?
- How? What is needed?

Please introduce yourself and tell me about your organisation in general. What is your vision and aim?

My name is De Paul I'm a graduate in Engineering Electronics & Communication form NIT Bhopal, and worked 2 years in Tata consultancy as a service programmer.

We started Yardstick 2 years back. The reason for starting was that we didn't like the way science is taught.

The interest in the subject is there, but the way it is taught is de-motivating. Also, we (the Yardstick founders) found we didn't fit in the job we were doing at that time. We all had an interest in education. My parents for example are teacher s themselves.

Initially, we were thinking- proper assessment in India is totally neglected. Any kind of board exam majorly measure memory skills only. Kids will only learn for memory, nothing else. Only the marks on paper count. Naturally understanding doesn't reward anything. So we wanted a benchmark for schools teaching and learning concept. We want them to really understand not generate knowledge and memory only. Kids should truly understand! Stating only Newton's law won't make you understand nature. Only if the children can discover it by themselves, it makes sense, and they'll develop ownership, when they really understand. It's a life skill we're developing. We want children to start questioning on everything that is happening around. You start questioning and then you go back and continue questioning each and everything. Science is a set of skills not only concepts.

So we started by trying out a few things. We realised there is a huge gap between objectives of science teaching and what the outcome is. We put up a test and the children hardly scored 10 % of what was asked. Practical learning was lacking.

Now our idea is: experiential learning! People learn from experience. You take the children through a process of experience, and then I don't have to tell them the law, they'll just learning by experience. That's what we wanted to support. Initially we only tried out. For example I like experiments, but will kids like that also? Do they get bored, or would they like to learn?

Textbook teaching is like this: It will state the law and even if there is an experiment explained it will also give the answer. That is not an experiment! If you already know what is going to happen. You need to do it and find it out by yourself. So we developed a set of experiments for the kids.

See, even good schools with reasonably good labs, they're not reaching their full potential. The reason why kids run away from labs is that there are big equipments that kids are afraid of. Kids don't feel part of it. We wanted to use things which are really around. Things you can see everywhere. What is there in the life around us and then create attachment to the laws. Why do you need a seatbelt when you are driving your car? Explain the law but also make them understand it saves your life.

Then we noticed something in a school. We realised each child is equally creative and bright. It is just the way they are brought up or how they have been taught in school which is making a difference. If the kid is not able to learn than that is the teachers fault, not the kids fault. What they do not realise: each kid has their own ways of understanding. Some learn very easily just by reading, others need a logical connection in order to understand. When you have a logical connection between things that is when you really learn things and start understanding things.

What is your strategy? How do you address and reach your target audience?

We started with 30 kids in a government school. We had some problems with English, but what we realised also is we had a communication gap because they are seeing the principal in front. After a while they loosened up and we became very friendly. What happened is we started with 30 kids, in 3 weeks, with an open invitation to all kids; we had around 100 kids joining us in the end. The most interesting part was the way they looked at science all together. They need more visual. They are taught the law and told 'Just believe what I'm telling you' by a teacher. So they won't remember. These kids started really relating things and improving also on the communication level.

See, kids are afraid to ask questions. There are so many obvious things around and we should be as brave as Newton to ask WHY? In India in early ages this culture is created that you are not allowed to ask questions. So if you ask, that means your not understanding. But it's the other way around! To ask a question you need to understand a lot of things. What we were trying to do is to promote questioning. You don't accept things just the way they are, you need to ask and you need to have a good reason for it. A lot of interesting questions came up from the students, which even I hadn't thought of before. When a good question comes that's when you know that kids have understood something.

Why do you think children are discouraged from asking questions?

Teachers themselves lack a lot of understanding and it is shown in the answers they give. There is a very basic difference. For science you need a lot of knowledge. Things keep changing, new things come up. See the way teachers are educated. Someone asking me a question is challenging. If I don't know the answer I get frustrated. I don't want to look as if I don't have a lot of knowledge. So when we go around with this hands-on-learning idea, there are a lot of questions coming up. Even I don't find answers every time. You should be enough open minded and you should not have doubt. The kid is not trying to test you or offend you. They are just trying to learn and are curious. Curiosity is a basic for our lives, it is what distinguishes us from animals, I think.

I have to prepare for this kind of questions, which requires a lot of extra effort. What I think teachers lack is motivation. Why should I take the extra effort it doesn't matter to them if one teacher maybe teaches this way and another one maybe teaches a better way, in the end they are paid the same money. They receive the same respect or appreciation. The principal may appreciate if kids are scoring more marks. But for scoring more marks you don't have to answer every doubt of the child. You just need to mug up what is in the textbook. So teachers really stress on completing the syllabus and making sure kids write what it says in the textbook.

One typical example is, a child not giving the exact answer in a test, as it was in the textbook. So the teacher decides not to give a mark, because he did not state the law 1 to 1. Actually, the child had the right understanding and just put it in his/her own words. Now a kid who has the right understanding but doesn't state it as it is in the textbook gets not rewarded with good marks, but someone quoting the law exactly but probably not really understanding it, will get a good mark. There is something wrong about that, isn't it? As a teacher what would I prefer? As a teacher I want them to score marks. Any other effort is not at all rewarded.

The thing is whenever we tell teachers, science can be taught in a much better way (of course we don't tell them so directly) it doesn't sound feasible for the principals, the management or the teachers. They think it takes a lot more effort and time to do. Teachers will not be able to do it; kids will only play but not learn. There are a lot of misconceptions. So at first we will just show them that it is possible.

Did you need approval from the principals? What is your approach? Did you get him on board and then everyone else was ok with it? Who did you address?

As far as schools in India concern there are not many decision makers. First we go and tell the principal: "Let us show you what we do". We take one class in the classroom and the teachers and principals see what we are doing. If they are happy with that they'll go along with it.

We went to one school and proved how easily it can be done. We taught the children and the teachers came to watch. Usually what happens for one law the teacher would take 6-7 sessions, where the law is constantly repeated and the kids would read it out loud- 7 sessions only for memory classes!

Our approach is not to tell e.g. Newton's law. We use activities, and experiments, we demonstrate and discuss with the kids. Once the kids come out with the understanding by themselves, then we name it as Newton's law. The kids discover it and they get the joy of discovery. That's when the have fun and enjoy coming to school.

Attempt: if you want to expand and reach towards more schools you cannot directly interact with the children, it should be you interacting with the teachers and training them. We're looking at enabling a school, to doing it on their own. First years we'll be training the teachers we'll go along with them. In the second and third years they do it independently. And, say, in the fourth year they'll come up with their own activities. It takes some time to enable teachers and getting them to doing it on their own. So this year, we're training teachers making teachers part of the activities and taking them along.

What are their concerns? What are the obstacles and challenges you face?

First, sometimes schools get offended. The thing is in a way, it looks like I'm coming in telling you "Your not teaching the right way, I'm going to tell you how to do it right". They are in the business for a long time, and this approach might be offending. Some of the international schools say: "We have the best teachers and the best approach, we pay our teachers so and so much, what extra can you do?" Some people take it in ego and that is the challenge. But most schools take it in a positive way. We have 90 % of conversion. They are accepting the thing and the whole idea of doing it. So it's not much of a challenge. See, management itself is pretty open for a change. Now, the problem is, how do you motivate teachers to this part of it. We go to the schools once in a week. But it has to be a very regular part of curriculum; it cannot be only a few weeks. We do lots of discussions and kids like to have the same discussions every class. If it doesn't happen, the kid's interest in a normal class goes down. The situation will become worse. We'll need to make sure teachers take it forward. It doesn't happen in one week. The parents should also support the idea. If the kids go back and ask something at home they should spend time and explain and accept the asking. Support from the teachers as well as parents are equally important. I personally feel that more learning happens at home than at school.

The teachers have a lot of problems. You cannot blame them for lack of care or respect for the kids ... nothing like this is there. Just for you to get a feel of it: Whoever didn't get any other job has probably joined teaching or thought of teaching as a profession.

How much do teachers in India earn on average?

Private schools: 5,000-6,000 Rupees/ month. It varies with experience and the type of school.

If it's a government job they are paid better. The irony is: the government pay maximum salary. There are not many good government schools. The selection process also is not a very clean process.

Let's say I'm a good teacher and I'm in the middle of a set of lazy teachers. Nobody cares about me and the quality of the teaching I do. Nobody questions you.

If it is in a private school, parents pay hefty fee for their child a year and if their child is not getting good education the parent will go to the school and shout at the principle.

In government schools who is going to question? Whatever you do, you are free to do. They are paid 10,000-15,000 Rupees/month, more than any school would be able to afford. The problem is, since there is nobody to question and nobody to care then that's how government teachers naturally get into doing anything. There is no control! They plan 1 lesson for one year and they keep teaching that for the next 30 years.

So what we do is asking them to take a total change to their lesson. Why should anyone do that? Teachers have a lot of work to do: Every two or three weeks they have a test, 6hrs of teaching every day. A teacher has 4-5 classes, which adds up to 200 students and 200 papers to correct. Then they have to get it signed from the parents, so much homework for the teachers.

They have school from 9-3 after that meetings, and the administrative work is a lot, collect the fees, correct the papers, distributing the textbooks, address the parents, making progress reports. It's a lot of work, not very interesting work as well. After some time, naturally you get bored. It's the same monotonous work every year.

Are there any after-school activities?

In international schools, there will be yoga, any kind of sports and one major trend is also coaching for IITs. Every parent wants their kid to be an IIT engineer. The pressure starts right from 5th class. The coaching is undertaken by third parties, not from schools, but in the premises of the schools.

Another major problem is in attrition. Teachers don't stay at the same school for very long. The reason is 80-90% of teachers are women. They get married have a husband and stop working after marriage. I don't see any kind of loyalty towards the school. School is not putting in any effort to improve the teacher's situation. If a teacher gets offered a better payment she/he just moves on to the next one. There is a lot of cycling of teacher happening. On average a teacher would stay only 2-3 years in one school. We train them, and every time I see new faces. We put in all the effort and then the teacher goes. They usually do not continue at the other school and we have to start all over again.

30-40% of teachers keep changing every year. Nothing changes in a day. Training a teacher takes some time- it takes some 2-3 years. All our effort is gone waste. That's why even schools put not any effort in training teachers. If you train a teacher, and she/he becomes more efficient then she/he changes to a good school.

Why are you taking this approach and not start where the teachers are getting trained to become teachers?

We are still a start up. It is true what you are saying, that would be ideal. What we are trying to do is collaborate with one of the collages, getting into BEd (Bachelor of Education), by interact with them and making them part of what we do. Now again associating with a degree college is a little difficult. You need to show a lot of credibility. We are just a start up organisation, besides, we are a private organisation.

If you are a NPO, or NGO they'll be more welcoming. If you are a private body they don't give you a chance so easily.

So why are you a private organisation?

I've seen a lot of NGOs work and worked with them privately and there are some exceptionally well run NGOs. Yet, generally in an NGO what happens if you are not working for profit, how do you get motivated? Do you think everybody is so selfless? No there are no selfless people like that. Nobody has a responsibility. It is a NGO, if it closes down nobody is responsible. Somebody else is giving them funding. "Take 1 Lakh Rupee[11] and do something with it". Now what they do with that money is up to them. But as a private organisation, if I don't do well schools won't come to me, kids won't be happy, parents aren't happy. So if I want to earn my bread and butter I have to do well. There is something that keeps us running. I don't see anything wrong about making profit with doing good and being responsible. We just wanted to make sure there is some motive. My salary right now is much less than two years ago, so we're not driving for profit. But there should be some motive. We give something to schools and teachers and get a good feedback. That's a good incentive.

That's what is lacking in the schools. There is no incentive for the teachers. If you want to give incentives, morally, keep them motivated. So for these things you need to be a private organisation. NGOs are controlled by the organisation that funds them. We want to work in a free working environment. It gives a little extra motivation and people put in more effort.

In the future what needs to change, what can be done?

See I got a feeling that things are changing, at least here. Looking at the response, the first year was pretty tough and we saw many sceptical faces. Now they are showing happy faces. So the response is positive. What we're trying to do right now, is getting into the government schools, particularly.

We have a couple of government schools, but the whole thing involves a cost. We are teaching hands-on which includes materials and hence a cost for providing it for each child. Right now why we are not able to get into the government schools is we don't have any funding. Nobody is sponsoring us and plus we cannot give it for free. It's quite some amount of money. Each activity will cost you at least 30-40 Rupees. That's quite an amount. One attempt is to bring down the cost. Currently, we're just trying for alternatives, like material that can be used. We're trying to bring down the cost to a considerable level that government schools can afford, trying to make it cheaper and cheaper so that it can be affordable by a lot more students.

And currently how are you making profit?

---

[11] 1 Lakh Rupees = 100,000 Rupees

We are sort of break even. We charge for training and the activity including the material we use. Except of in the first session, where we'll give it for free.

Doesn't it take lots of convincing? If it is not for free and you're telling them to teach in a different way?

See, one good thing [smiles a little mischievously], at least for us, is the competition between schools. Now the private schools in CBSE they have taken away the exams. At the national board there are no more exams, there is no more mugging up. That's why I'm saying things are changing positively. Since there are no more exams, there are no more marks. There are only grades. The children get grades for the overall performance over the year, e.g. on how they discuss in the classroom. It's quite a change. Therefore, under the National Board government schools are really stressing activity-based learning. Teaching should include some activities. This is new for the schools so they need some help and that's where we come in.

This is introduced by the government, by the ministry? Yes.

And how are they going to measure the performance of the kids?

How I see it, assessment should be continuous. There should not be one final exam at the end of the year only. There will be small projects given, you might do some small research in the classroom, discussions, report writing and based on all that the mark will be given. It is a way where teachers interact more with the children and teachers can get that feedback on a continuous basis.

Do you think the teachers are ready?

Well, not yet. The thing is the textbooks, the CBSE textbooks, are quite improved. If you read through the National Curriculum Framework, they have designed the way it should be taught. That is pretty impressive. It's the same thing we are doing. We're trying to find out more or less, what it is you have to do in practice, and come up with a guideline plan. So they are not ready yet, but in a few years time, things would change.

Thank you very much Paul

A.2 Interview – Minhajuddin Farugi (Environmental Consultant)

Name of organisation   Independent Environmental Consultant
Name of Interviewee   Minhajuddin Faruqi
Date: 21/Jun/2010   Time: 18:30-20:00   Place: Project House, Banjara Hills, Hyderabad

Background to Minhaj:

- (Independent) Environmental Consultant
- PostGrad (MSc) in Environmental Science
- Worked at NGC, as well as 6 years for CEE, currently partner of WWF-India, AP
- Is about to start a private corporation
- Contact: +91(0)9849438388, minhajuddin.faruqi@gmail.com

Interview notes

- EE started with M.C. Mehta, Supreme Court Educationist in 1996, who said it should be compulsory from 1st class onwards
- Discussion aroused: should it be an extra subject or spread across all subjects
- 2004 NCERT developed NCTE framework and then ruled, the responsibility lies with the States
- Now: SCERT is responsible, and school's adopt EE based on NCERT framework
- Therefore, they did a lot of workshops with NGOs
- The decision was made it should be a separate subject, what books? → Activity book. Who should make them? → NGC: NGC Environmental Education Activity Books
- Different agents in AP working on EE:
    a) PCB: Pollution Control Board (government Body)
    b) WWF: with children in clubs, not with schools specifically, since 1980 in AP
    c) CEE: since 2000 in AP
    d) NGC: Central Government Program
    e) HMDA: Hyderabad Metropolitan Development Authority, e.g. cleaning of Buddha Lake, in cooperation with various partners
    f) BPP: Buddha Purnima Project, contact, IFS Officer: Akbar (23450359, 09989990756)

CEE

- Funds other NGOs
- Development of vegetable gardens for lunch, medical plants
- Campaign against plastics funded by multinational corporation
- Try to link activities with curriculum, identified chapters, and created link
- Funded by UNICEF, TATA, Government (SSA=Sarva Shiksha Abhiyan, All Education Program)
- Sponsors do auditing & monitor performance
- Urban, climate change related: 'Life and Conservation', working with 30-40 schools giving presentations, providing knowledge, combined with science experiments, manual on climate change
- Melting of glaciers and effect

- Approach: Teacher's training only, don't work directly with students

Problem: Intangibility

'Can you see Climate Change?' it is not tangible
Other topics, science projects, with immediate result, visible, link there, instant understanding

Problem Complexity, Novelty

People who want to educate and change society's behaviour need good knowledge of the topic. Relatively new, very scientific, not easy to grasps, all the aspects involved, problem of translating the topic into children's words

Problem: Financing

E.g. many international programs run online use TV as medium, in order to make this intangible topic more presentable to children. However, government schools do not have such kind of money, only high end international schools, or some rich private schools will be able to do that.

Problem: Difference in schools

- In Private Schools, success rates excellent, approach, tell principle you'll save so and so much money, they agree and force the teachers to do it
- ICSE, CBSE- EE is compulsory, have separate teacher for the subject, from 2010/20111 onwards
- SSC government & private – EE not compulsory, use NGC books, "but they are too wage"
- In government schools no monitoring, EE not compulsory, no marks, no motivation, no control, job for life with good payment, maybe transfer, if class results in terms of marks not good, no other incentives, also strong through unions
  School is from 8-4, 10 teachers are on role, but only 2 will be present, others doing private things, or run errands for principle.
- In government schools: no light, no fans, use daylight, 1 blackboard, 2 classes share I room (e.g. 9th & 10th), if there is one computer, it'll be locked away in the principles office so the children to not break it.
- 'At government schools the result was practically Zero'
  CEE project results only 30-40%, report provided by schools
- This year only 1,300 new teachers got a government teaching job, "Why is none of those an environmental education teacher?

Problem: Teacher's education at BEd

- Environmental education will be covered in 2nd semester of final year, but only textbook learning, students learn only concepts to pass the course, no idea what to do in practice with children

Climate Change – results measured by CEE

Good: uniqueness of topic, something new

Combined with scientific experiments, hands-on learning = more successful

Problem of funding: CEE funded for 9 years by TATA, last year started educating on climate change, but funding stopped

Internal discrepancy- more textbook approach, Minhaj didn't like, so he left

Successful program:

PARKS 2004-2006

Funded by MCH (Municipal Corporation Hyderabad)$\rightarrow$ 1,300,000 Rs, 2, 500,000Rs

Got students to come to parks in walking distance every 2nd Saturday for 1.5 hrs to learn from and in the parks

Provided education material, hand-outs/guidelines, every group working on different topic & next day in school during assembly in the morning had to present it so others, so they'll learn also

2nd year: plantation in schools (problem: not all schools have land, but they kept some plants in the room at least)

Final aim: start your own garden, or have a few plants at home

Success factors:

- Uniqueness of project, was something new
- Teachers will go out and learn, liked not being in the classroom
- Good material provided by CEE
- Strong monitoring of activities undertaken by teachers through CEE people, who went to schools during weekdays and got their feedback and results
- CEE was giving out prices to the winners, best performers
- Training for teachers in National Parks
- Overall motivation by everyone was high, great responses

Problem:

Management at MHC changed, new person not in favour of the programme $\rightarrow$ no more funding

On other NGOs:

- SSA, mainly working on literacy, getting village kids to go to school, also TV channel from 4-6 o'clock, CLIPS= good. Problem: Environmental program was cancelled, funded NGOs for 5-6 years, but don't believe in concept of NGOs anymore
- WWF: work directly with kids, forming clubs, focus on climate change per se!
- PEAS: Program for Environmental Awareness in Schools
- Media: channel showing EE by NCERT: every Sunday 1hr, in English & Hindi, funded by UGC: universal grants commission
- Times of India: Online measure on Carbon Footprint, problem: for middle class people only! "How often do you fly", needs to be localised $\rightarrow$ done by CEE, in their ANNUAL REPORT

- IYCN (Indian Youth Climate Network) working with WWF, initiated by WWF? iycn.org, working on climate change

Trend:
Towards ESD (Education for sustainable development) includes economic aspects "You'll save this and this much money if you behave like this"

A.3 Interview – W.G. Prasanna Kumar (National Green Corps)

Name of organisation   National Green Corps (NGC) Andhra Pradesh
Name of Interviewee   W.G. Prasanna Kumar (Director)
Date: 28/Jun/2010   Time: 10:00-12:00   Place: NGC Office Hyderabad

Please tell me about your organisation in general. What is your vision/aim?

NGC was constituted in 2001 by the Ministry Environment and Forrest (Government of India). Before that I was in the Pollution Control Board. We were doing a program called "Hyderabad Children's Environmental Science Congress" (HCESC) since 1998, which also conducted workshops for teachers. At the end of the workshop we asked their feedback. They said: "The workshop is very good, but whatever you said, we knew". And they asked "What is it we can do?" If you are interested in doing something that is good. Rather than just knowing. Considering that experience, next year I went alone doing the trainee programs for teachers. It was in 7 districts in Andhra Pradesh (AP), followed by again the HCESC. By then it was called "AP Children's Environmental Science and Action Congress" (APCESAC), so action also. It was very well taken in the 7 districts.

After that the Environmental Minister of the Union Government Body here called for a conference of the parliamentarians on environment. They had conducted it in Hyderabad, and I showed him my documentation. "Something like this is very interesting and it's happening in AP. Do you think it can be done everywhere in India". Within 10 days I got a letter that they want to draft a program for which they need somebody from AP to come. So I went there, and along with me e.g. CEE and WWF; and by evening we drafted a small program of "Eco-Clubs". That was put in front of the Environmental Ministers of all states and the union ministers they had a conference and decided they wanted to do it in 565 districts in the country. So in 5,750 schools the "Eco Club" program was initiated in AP. They sent a letter to every state government. Since I am keen on this I pushed it and we got the order released by the state government. I was still with the Pollution Control Board by that time. So we were the first state to constitute the National Green Corps in terms of actual field level grounding. Within three months we grounded it. On 05/Jun/2001 NGC started in AP, on World Environment Day. And 20/Jun/2010 our first program of plantation started.

While we were doing this I was in touch with the ministry, I was in touch with the education also, since the program is conducted in the education most of the time in the schools. By the time NGC was born, WWF had gone to standstill and CEE was not there yet. CEE came up in this place a little later. It was like empty space nobody interested in doing anything. So we gave small money 1,000 Rs to each school. We did extensive training programs. We picked up people who are keen on doing something in the streets. That was a huge success. I went to each of the 23 districts and did training programs for 100 teachers.

When we were doing this the chief minister at that time got excited by the way we were doing the program, so he lifted it up to 9,000 high schools. This was a huge task! At the International Ozone Day (IOD) conducted in AP, Hyderabad for the Gov of India by the Gov of AP one child mentions the program is called "The National Green Corps" and we have a parallel program called "The National Cadets Corps" if you give similar support it will get pushed to a very high level. So then the Chief Minister made an announcement that there will be a separate directorate of APs NGC and the children will be given the value and status equal to NCC and they'll be given a certificate which will have a value. Not yet fulfilled. 10 years later. But NGC directly came in and made an announcement on the directorate that day and it took 2.5 years for the people in power to mall it over and finally give an order.

By then we were trying to push the program scale to 9,000 high schools, secondary schools. In AP right from the beginnings I was very keen on doing something very concrete. I am the only social scientist in this program in the country. Others are all scientists and technologists. So for me more than knowledge, what is important is the action. Knowledge always has been secondary for me. What is happening in the field is more important than what is happening in the brain. I've always pictured it as a program done in the field rather than a program delivered in the classroom. There's a difference how we conducted it to how others conducted it. I wanted children to get a benefit. So we were always mulling on how to make the child do something and give a record of what the child has done and equate it to National Cadets Corps. If you want to do something like this you need to be really clear about which classes and schools are you dealing with. There should be some criteria. In AP we have restricted it to 8th and 9th class. It's a 2-year program. Initially, I was planning to have 20 children joining in 8th, each year. So you'll have a NGC unit of 20 children from 8th class and then in the second year 20 children in 9th class in each school. I didn't like the word 'club' at any point of time. I always pushed it as National Green Corp 'unit'. In the very beginning this program was called as national green Army, which was also mentioned on books and certificates we gave out! Later on I believe there was some objection taken by army so they changed it to Green Corps.

So you do give out certificates? I thought you mentioned the NGC wasn't on the same level as NCC.

We started giving out certificates, to have something rewarding for the kids, giving value to it, having marks, there were points given for each activity. So we wanted the teachers to mark it based on the participation of the children. By the time it has taken roots we had a big judgement coming in from the supreme court of India. It said that environment education is compulsory and for all levels. So when it is compulsory at all levels I thought that is a big opportunity to work at all levels. Big work and great work and not restricted. So I started working on every class. Class 1-10, university- everything was available to me and I was really thrilled. So we made activity book for class 1-10 and we also made activity book/ textbook for plus 1 plus 2 (11th 12th standard). I didn't want a burden on the child. We devised activity book in English and Telugu, very simple subject in that. It became a compulsory textbook for 11 and 12. While I was doing that I got in contact with NCERT, whatever I was doing I was doing in contact with school education department, with higher education department, with college education, with university, with professors, all of them together. At that time I even had the idea of pushing it into engineering colleges, I started working on green buildings, energy conversation for each sector of engineering I wanted to have some subject which is really linked to their life. So it was a huge amount of work. Then I came back to schools gain.

My research focus is on schools only.

What we did got adopted by the states department, it was a great success. 8,9,10 classes took it over (SSC) and printed the book. But they're not doing anything about that, there just giving the book, I came to know. So I said this will not work, and we went back to ground level, we'll do the work with the schools only. Let me leave all other work, because at ground level if I have nothing happening, if I'm just talking I'm just spreading, extension will not work, unless I have extensive work at the field level, so then we went back.

We saw training programs for teachers as our capability, because going to the schools, more than 20,000 high schools, out of which I'm dealing with 5,750 schools, initially I went to 9,000 schools, I said I cant deal with this big number, so let me get it down to a manageable number. So I pushed it down to 5,750 which is the requirement of Ministry for Environment and Forest.

How many schools did you deal with in Hyderabad only?

In Hyderabad we are working with 250 schools. In greater Hyderabad it is 400 schools. But that doesn't mean anything. It just means the number. We did the training program across the state continuously but we wanted to know what is happening to our training program in the field. And we do not have a method of going to every school. With 5 staff members is not possible to go to 5000 schools. Their capacity maximum is to reach about 25 schools in a month, each of them. So we introduced NGC student's environmental congress. I removed 'science' and action from it, because the moment you have science, only the science teacher comes in. The science teacher doesn't know how to do work. He can only talk concepts. Doing work is something different, it is digging a pig and planting a tree, it is physical work, which the science teacher is not very keen on. He is only teaching in the classroom, he is the boss of the classroom, not of the school. So if he wants to do something like that he needs permission of the principle to leave the classroom.

So we started calling it NGC student's environmental congress. Every year we'll have schools come back, which selected 2-3 children with a teacher in a group of 50 schools each they converge and discuss what they did - students/school projects they did. Again we selection from this group and had a program at the state level.

But all the schools are not the same (Telugu, Hindu, Christian, Muslim missionary, Medium Schools, State government, ICSE, CBSE). I do not have any restriction on going to this type of school or that type of school. Everybody is the same for me, because I'm looking at the child doing something at the field. Behaviour pattern change is my concern. So for each group I had a training program, I had bishops coming there, sitting there, in the program, telling this is a good work, you do it. I was just trying to see that whatever influence mechanism is available use that and get it done at the field level.

So you had a different strategy for the different schools?

For each school stream, yes. ICSE is the only group which introduced EE compulsory, including textbooks and exams. This applies only to this small group. But at this time what happened NCERT started backtracking. They were changing government of India. The new director for NCERT said, I don't want the old syllabus, I don't want EE compulsory. So instead of giving it as a separate salad, I want the salad to be part of a curry or bhiriany of education. So he made the salad part of the bhiriany. That is called as infusion strategy. CEE is the father of infusion strategy. They introduced that environment should be a part of every subject, and not a separate subject.

Do you disagree with EE not being taught as a separate subject?

I 100 % disagree with that. I consider infusion as confusion. It's like salt available in every dish, but to what effect? I'm looking at behaviour change. Salt can be put in every dish, we may agree that, but salt cannot be put in milk, salt cannot be put in sweet dish. Everybody will object, "No not this much of salt, only a certain amount of salt". Salt is a very minute thing. Do you have salt as a separate item, or do you have it infused?

So NCERT director wanted to do something which was different from the earlier director. The earlier one was a rightist; this one was a leftist, now there is no director at all. So the new one along with CEE, NCERT designed the "National Curricula Framework" 2005. This one is completely different from the way we have transacted the curriculum till that time. It is about constructing the world view. Reality is constructed by the child in course of interaction with reality.

This is a huge shift in terms of how we did education earlier, how we did education. This is like a democratic participative education. Earlier one was like fugal given education. Earlier education is memory based, reproduction based, repetition based. But this is like creative, innovative, experimental. The system is not ready, but the policy is there. It was given 2005 and they said to implement it. According to that policy, environment education is infused into every subject. For example, in maths you would teach so much of water is coming in, so much of water is getting out- that is environmental education for them, because it is about water leakage. In English language, somewhere you have a beautiful text about a tree, that's how you get environmental education into the mind of the child. That is the conception in the newly created methodology. Anyway somehow I am criticising my on system in front of a foreigner I am aware of that, but I'm being self critical.

When you want to prepare food, will you prepare food, or will you prepare the cook first? What is your answer?

Could you please explain, why you think the system is not ready?

So we have the curriculum in place, we do not have teachers in place. Curriculum framework for pupil's education was given in 2005, but the National Curriculum Framework for teacher's education has come in 2009 only. If I am a person who is devising a strategy, I would first have the framework for the teachers, so that teachers are ready and then the ready teachers go to the students and give it.

These confused teachers, what sort of infusion can they do? What sort of education can they do? Anyway that's how we work as a system. Here you have the NCF- do it. Now we are saying teachers will get trained. We are just saying now. We are not yet doing it.

Since I'm also doing my PhD in environmental education I am also keen on this whole process. We are dealing with education department and environment department. Each district as an Institute of education and training, this is where the primary teachers get trained and come out. Yet, it is confusing, again. We think that if we have primary school teachers training centre that's ok, that is enough. We do not have secondary school teacher training institutions. What we have for secondary school teachers is BEd colleges. But there is no district structure there. In some districts you have the college run by the education department, in some it is run by the universities. So there is no linkage between all that and the people who give the input for the teacher training institution. They gave orders, but if they are not insisted they are not implemented. Just because you have an order, doesn't mean it gets implemented. This work that I have done as far as curriculum, interaction, no other NGC in the country has done. Everywhere else they're focussing on eco clubs.

This is also my biggest discussion with CEE, that the concept of infusion doesn't make any difference. If it had made a difference, do I see a dustbin in the school? Do the children put their waste only in the dustbin? Is there a method by which school or children are taking care of plantation or the energy is conserved and waste is managed in the school? If nothing like that is established, all your knowledge, concepts is useless for me. It is just a dream.

Anyway they are fond of that, because they can sit in a big conference room, with big academician, as part of the infusion group. The problem is, if you go by infusion method, teachers will not allow you to touch the traditional content of subjects.

A separate subject would make sense. I agree with you, if its part of every subject the teacher will probably not be so keen on stressing environmental issues.

Yes, exactly. So this is what I am discussing with NCERT. The problem is, if you do not evaluate, the child and teachers won't do it. It is fancy to have environmental education. It is easy to talk, but if it is not compulsory, if I have 100 things to do, then I will leave it. 90 % of the people may leave it. But do you believe that environmental education is required or not. If this is required will you make it optional? That is my question!

I am in touch with the lawyer who has gone to court on this particular subject. I've given my books to him. I've told him that activity generates activity. Knowledge generates knowledge.

So the 2005 framework is more knowledge based and focused on concepts. Are there any activities?

No it is not like that. 2005 framework is activity based, but 2005 curricula framework, while they were doing the activity based curricula framework, they have infused environment subject, which means activity.

Anyway last year they came back saying that, we will have exemplar environmental projects also, we will have grading also, that grading will be separate grading and it will show up in the progress card also. Whatever I discussed with them long back, now they are saying they will do it. But then they have confused the total system in the country in such a way that they sent a letter saying that we're going to the supreme court on this aspect and we are appealing to the Supreme Court for changing this. When you say I am appealing to the Supreme Court and changing this, and you are talking to the person who is implementing something. What will he do? Will he implement or will he wait for the appeal?

Wait for the appeal.

Exactly! That is how they destroyed the environmental education in the country. And I straight away blame CEE for this confusion. CEE has a vested interest in retaining its space in the education sector, because they got huge money. My only concern is, in education people do not know how to handle environmental education. You give a handholding support initially, you get them to make their own internal structures, build expertise. Over a period of time they'll take over. Why should you be always present and always hold their hand? If you hold the child's hand always, it will be physically handicapped.

The education department in the country has more than a crore of employees. In this state itself they have 3 lakh teachers. At any point of time the environmental department or CEE or NGC none of us can ever match their numbers. They are huge. Public sector education is the biggest employer in this country. We have 92,000 schools in AP primary, upper primary and high schools. It is mind bobbling to think of one person reach even 1 day into that school from any other department except the education department. 92,000 mandates, where are you going to get 92,000 mandates from any department?

So my point is that you train the teachers. We are now speaking English but your mother tongue is definitely German. Would I have an interpreter for you throughout your life of research or will I train you in English so that you'll talk to me in English? But the strategy of CEE is that: you are a German, don't waist your time in learning English, I will give you an interpreter. So you will be permanently dependent on me.

That is the same with WWF also, isn't it? They do not deal with teachers and work directly with the children?

WWF is a fancy program. Let's not even discuss that because they are very small, miniscule. WWF reaches 100 schools out of 1 lakh schools, how does it matter? And 100 schools, 50 children or 20 children, and all elite schools. How does it matter? It doesn't make any difference. It has no effect. Except that it has the effect of coming in the media, because they are fancy big schools elite schools, well bread well read. It can come in the media any time, since they can speak English, and go at conference at higher levels. They have the advantage.

I'm not denying the role of either WWF or CEE or any other organisation. Each of them has their role. For instance, I am dealing with a program, of course I am also dealing with these elite schools, but elite schools are like pampered children. I cannot deal with a pampered child, because I have 5,750 in number. I can't pamper any school, but WWF can. They can take care of them very nicely deal with them properly. That is not possible for me.

WWF is anyway not bothered about this Supreme Court judgement and the decisions. They are not bothered.

CEE is bothered to some extent. They are an organisation build on the crippled education system. The system needed somebody's support. So CEE needs to show all the time that "You need our support, keep us in."

CEE has entered into AP with the project support from Rattan Tata Trust and they pulled some NGOs and they trained them, and trained the children. Number one: They dealt with 6th and 7th standard, whereas I dealt with 8th and 9th class. So they wanted to match at a lower level, so that there is no competition or conflict there. Number two is they are dealing through NGOs, whereas I was dealing through the structures. Mine is a different thing altogether. So they did the program as long as they got the support, and now there is no support so their program doesn't exist today. CEE doesn't have a school program. CEE, which is basically school education based program, has gone into different things in AP, like non-pesticide agriculture, because there was money there. They went into various things dealing with the Hussain Sagar lake and the surroundings. They are more into material development. There is a structure available in AP so they can tailor make material at any time. They have a huge structure of designers and material developers, who make material for the pollution control board. That's how they are still there and that material goes into the system, some way or the other once in a while. But they don't have a structured program for the schools presently.

My position on the other hand concentrates on structure, because structure is going to be there even if am not. If I go out, I will not go the child for more than 1 day in a year and that out of 5,750 schools. My capacity is 10 schools only, 1 day each. It's nothing. I will never be able to make any difference. So if I still want to make a difference I have to address the teachers system itself.

So how exactly does your approach look like?

I do not require people who believe in knowledge, who do not believe in attitude. We need to change habits. Just because you know everything, doesn't mean you can do it now. So I require a batch of people who will exactly think like me. These people are the physical education teachers, because they are into play and in play there is not theory. There may be a theory in play which is also there, but when they are playing the game, or learning the game, they are not going by the theory.

Whatever the physical education teachers say, they say to every child. They are not restricted to 50 children who are eco club members. They can get a system implemented in the school. If he says "Don't litter", he is meaning that anywhere in the school, by any person in the school, any time in the school. This is possible only through my physical education teacher because every child will go and tell him: "good morning sir". Even if he doesn't play, he will say "Good morning sir" or if he meets him on the street looking a different direction, he will go in front of him and say "Good morning sir". I mean the fellow who physically beats children in the school. Physical education teacher in course of training children he will beat them, but still children will go and tell: "good morning sir". Because they think he is the person who is interested in them. He is committed to the game. He is committed that the child learns how to play the game.

So I am going through the physical education teacher asking them, plant some trees in the school, let not any child litter. If there is any leaking tap make the children responsible for that. Be the boss of the school, be the boss of environment in the school. He is not only the boss of environment in the school building but also in the school playground. Nobody else is interested in the playground in the school, except the physical education teacher. Nobody is interested in the compound wall of the school, the outside wall nobody is interested except him. He is interested in the total building and all citizens, all children in the school.

Is he naturally the boss, or is that what you want him to be?

Naturally he is the person who rules the school assembly. Children fall in line with his whistle- 1000 children, 1 whistle. If he says no where anywhere litter in the school we'll have to follow it. He is not a class teacher. Science teacher is a class teacher. He belongs to some classes to which he goes. Other children will not go and say good morning to him. But for the physical education teacher, even if he is not taking any class they will go and say: "Good morning sir". Even if they are not playing the game, they will go and say hello. And I require an authority, a discipline, and environmental discipline to be pushed in. The physical education teachers drill. That type of drill should be there. So I have children performing the drill in a band. It looks like a band, it looks like marching, but what I am instilling is: accepting it on demand and following a command. Accepting a command and following a command, would look like dictatorship, would look not democratic. In fact it would look fascist, would look not considerable for the latest model of society. But the latest model of civil society across the world, which is developed, follows this. They will not throw litter anywhere, they will not say "this is democracy so you can throw your litter anywhere" on the face, in somebody's face or in somebody's house also. No. it's a dictatorship there as far as waste management is concerned. Across the world, in all developed countries it is dictatorship. But our people enjoy talking about democracy.

So form environmental awareness I went to environmental action, from environmental action now I have gone to environmental discipline. Now I am saying, no more environmental awareness, no more environmental action, but environmental discipline.

How do you train the physical education teacher? He must have some conceptual knowledge to fulfil the role you assign to him.

No theory on plants, germination, seed, knowledge about environment, global warming, green house effect, all those things happening.

Mustn't he also know what he/she can do in the field. I think people don't even know all the things that can be done in practice to protect the environment.

Did you read any English novel? *For example Harry Potter* .OK you read Harry Potter. Did you learn your alphabets first, or Harry Potter first?*My alphabets.*

So I am talking about alphabets in environmental education.

So that's what NGC is doing then? They are telling them the alphabets?

Yes, because society is not even literate. When the society is not even literate, make them to learn alphabets and small words.

The alphabets, that's what I consider as knowledge also.

I am talking about ABC of work! I am not talking about ABC of knowledge on that. Because I tried knowledge route, 10 years, all levels from medical education to primary schools. Now I find that all this is useless and in the end you or somebody else will come and ask me: "You have been working in the environment sector for the past 10 years, show me one school, where I can see whatever you are saying is happening" Out of 5,750 schools which I am dealing with, I don't have 1 school which is following this.

You are an outsider. You don't even know what I am going through. You will come after 20 years of my life and tell me: "Useless fellow, you didn't do anything. Nothing is happening. You are only talking." That's what the world is going to say. That's what the world has said to me! Show me one school. What school I can show? I'm afraid of showing any school, because I don't know. The students I trained have gone. That teacher I trained got transferred. School management also changed. I can't tell to you with confidence, you go and check this particular school, you will find this happening.

If I do an analysis of my own life at the end, in 13 years of service I have not done anything. I can only say that I got my salary every month I did whatever I did every month. When I give marks to my life I get 0 out of 100, because it's not happening in the field. Action in the field is important, not knowledge. All these people will go to their graves with their knowledge, it's useless for me. Graveyard will have the knowledge.

How are the physical education teachers taking it so far?

There is scepticism and resistance in them. However, the advantage is that last year, some 3000 physical education teachers are recruited new. So they have not yet tasted the leisure of life in the school. So them we caught. Fresh, any change easy, when there is a change. When the change is happening, at that time you intervene. I told them:" You are officers. Others call you a teacher only, even a useless teacher, you create problems only for them" But I am saying: "You are the solution, not the problem; you are an officer, an NGC officer". I gave them a designation and told them that they are the boss out of 5,750 schools that we are dealing with maybe around 500 schools they are doing something.

And is there any control? Did you set them goals?

Yes. Goals are very clear. At the end of the year I'm not looking at something happening as a structure or environmental outcome there. I am looking at the school's total greenery being taken care of, the energy and water being taken care of. Anytime anybody coming to the school, they should be able to see. Out of the 5,750 school, go to 500 you will find it- anytime.

Since when are you implementing this strategy?

Since 6 month it's happening across the state. So now instead of doing the teacher training what we did before, I have put my staff to go to the school. Talk to the children in the school, talk to the teacher and the headmaster in the school. 5 people are reaching some 60 schools on average, in a month in a year they'll be going to 500/600 schools. If you ask me what is the level of success? I will say less than 1 %. It is very difficult to digest this answer called "less than 1 %". Nobody will give this answer. Everybody will say 30-40 % success. Even if you go by the modest fellow he will say 30 %. But I would say less than 1 %. I know the task in front of me.

Do you need any incentives for the teachers?

Incentives for the teachers are required, as well as student's incentives. I am already giving incentives to the teachers. Out of the 2,500 Rupees we have given to the school 500 rupees should be taken by the person who is managing it. 2500 rupees is a very little amount in a year. I know that it is nothing. But still I am saying I am recognising you, I am not giving you money.

In a parallel program like this in NCC they give 800 Rupees per month. Our program should grow like that. I'm definite this will happen one day or the other. There will be some internal or external pressure. The physical educations teachers are really powerful .They are not like the science teacher, who will cripple at the classroom or somewhere, who will talk at the back of the principle. No, the physical education teacher will talk in front of the principle and confront him with what is happening. They can ask that question directly. They are audacious.

To my knowledge, I think it is in government schools, payment is ensured and there is no danger in loss of job, no matter what the performance of the teacher. Therefore, it is very hard to motivate them, to get them to do something else from what they've been doing for years.

You are 100 % right. That is the reality. That's why WWF doesn't focus on government schools at all. If you are a teacher not interested in teaching, will the children learn? They will! *Yes?* They will! They are interested in learning! You need to create an interest in the children, create incentives for the children. If I give 800 Rupees per month, still the teacher may not be interested in teaching. We need to give something to the child. If the child is not interested and the teacher is not interested, ok, the leave it. Don't address the work to them.

Interest the work to those people who are interested. If child is interested, but teacher is not, still the work can be done. If the teacher is interested, child is not, still you can do it. These are the two opportunities.

Therefore, my idea is to have a similar concept to the one of National Cadet Corps. Once you go through NCC, you will get a certificate, there is some grading. With that there is a preference in employment, which is why children go there. I want this similar preference to be given to the NGC children in forest employment and pollution control board employment. My vision for the future is, if you go through NGC with certain gradation with certain ranking with some accomplishment, having a background in NGC, you'll be given preference over other job applicants. For higher education in NCC if you did the program very effectively, you'll be given a certificate, so entry into higher education is also easy. I want that to be given to NGC children also because they should be recognised for the environmental work they have done.

So you think what children will learn from the physical education teacher is something they would also take home, if it becomes a habit at school level.

You are right. I believe that. Human beings say that 95 % of their life they think and act and only 5 % of their life they act and don't think. But what in fact 95 % of the time human beings don't think, they act. This is what I believe, but human beings say it is the other way around. This is the reality, and very difficult for human being to accept that "you don't think and act" human beings will not agree. But 95 % of human life is structured in such a way that it happens. It happens that you get up in the morning; it happens that you go to bed; it happens that you get married; that you eat. Whatever food you are eating, whatever dress you are wearing is just structured, so automatically you go take clothes from the closet, go to the loo. 95 % of your life you are not even thinking, it just happens. What do we focus on? Do we focus on thinking or action? *Action!*

So what you said is 100 % right. Environmental action requires habits, not knowledge, not environmental sense, not consciousness, no attitude is required here. I always believed right from the start that habits are required and habits should be formed. But I always thought that habits can be formed by telling. And then after a while I started thinking that habits can be formed by selling. Now I believe that habits can e formed by showing a habit and making people develop a habit. So structure a world like that

How many physical teachers are there per school? One only. Is she going to be able to control the whole area? Each classroom? Each light switch? Everything?

Suppose we have 10 children in the house. How many fathers are there? One only! But 10 children get controlled by 1 father. 1 sister, can she control? No. Science teacher is like the sister. Physical education teacher is like the father. Others will use the name of father and then they'll control. It is not the father who is controlling. Your older sister will tell you: "Hey I'll tell father, don't do this". The physical education teacher is a symbol of authority. Don't look at it as an individual who is doing the work. I don't expect him to do anything. I am only attaching my work to an authority, and making the authority say to the child, that this is your work. Don't think that he will go and check in every bathroom, every place, wherever. But if he is moving he is a symbol of discipline. This is my present hypothesis. My common sense says it is right. And we have to check it in the field which I will do in the next 6 month, 1 year.

Do you think you have a bit of an advantage that you are a government body and not an NGO?

We don't use the power of being a government. We go to the schools as a friend. They love us. Till now I have not used the government power. I do not go to them telling them I will take action against you.

What concern do schools have in regard to your new strategy?

Some concerns will be there, ok. Do whatever is possible. I know that I am not giving you financial rewards. I'm only telling you this, it is good to do. Do how much you can. I don't want you to talk, I want you to do. That is something which some schools are not able to digest. It is not talking but it is doing. A lot of people are interested in talking and writing. I say do something.

See I don't believe in these painting or dancing competitions. I've done all that. It's all useless, time pass time waste. The knowledge theory says that if a child is dancing and showing the expression than his/her attitude might have changed. But I found that children do not change their attitude. By the time they complete their dance you can find litter there in that room. Though it's nice to see good performance, but it's useless.

Habit is cultural; 90% of our behaving is cultural itself. Culture structures our life. Why not have environmental education structured like that? That's it. 10% violation will be there, people may not follow. Ok. We'll try to work on that.

Thank you so much for sharing your thoughts, Prasanna Sir!

A.4 Interview (e-mail) – Vanitha Kommu (Centre for Environment Education)

Name of organisation   Centre for Environment Education (CEE)
Name of Interviewee   Vanitha Kommu (Program Coordinator)
Date: 19/Jul/2010   Format: Set of questions send via e-mail

CEE background

*How many **employees** are there in the Andhra Pradesh team?*

The Andhra Pradesh Office team is about 10 and around 6 people work for schools education projects (not exclusively).

*What **schools** do you target? And why?*

Our major targets are the Government rural schools. There are 2 reasons:

1. Private schools usually can afford for additional activities like Environment Education where as Government schools can not.

2. The second is the numbers. If we can mainstream the Environmental Education (EE) in these schools through the department of education, the objective is achieved. Towards this we do demonstration projects in sample (which is 1,500, out to 15,000 government schools) with the help of local NGOs and selected teachers.

*What is the overall **aim** of projects conducted directly with schools?*
It is demonstrating the EE for mainstreaming. We work directly with some schools when the number is less (say 50). For projects with more numbers (say 150 -1,500) we take the help of local NGOs. Even though EE is the objective the components under each project will be different. For example: Water and sanitation education and actions, organic kitchen gardening, developing plantations, curriculum based environment educational activities, small projects on local environment etc.

*Who **takes decisions** on what programs to run?*
Even though conceptualisation is from CEE, there will be consultations and discussions with the stakeholders to be involved. But each CEE office is independent to take the decisions with guidance from other offices as and when required.

*What **support** do you need/get along the way (financial, human, operational)*
There are two areas where the support is required – one is finance and other is support from the government systems to run the project.

Nandanavanam project

Which schools did you target?
The target schools are with in 1-2 kms radius from an existing park so that students can visit frequently to conduct the activities. Around 23 schools are selected near 11 parks.

Is the project still ongoing? No.

Is the newsletter still created? Where do I find it? No. But if required I can share the old ones.

The suggestions given to the park, were they taken up?
Yes in some cases, but not widely. As you know there are several other factors involved.

Climate change teacher manual

Who was it given to (teachers of what school type)?
The manual was given to the teachers of 6th and 7th standards. All these are rural government schools.

How is it perceived?
This Climate change programme was introduced as part of the existing programme in all 1,500 schools with help of the manual and trainings during the year 2008. Apart from the existing activities it was felt important to introduce this due to emerging concerns.

Do you follow up if it's being used?
There is an internal reporting and monitoring system in the project design itself, where teachers have to send the report of the activities by the end of the academic year. Yes it was used.

Herbal gardens

Which type of schools did you target? Why?

Again rural government schools with sufficient land (1/10th of an acre), water and compound wall facilities which are necessary factors for success. Interest from the school towards participation was another criteria.

What response did you get?

Good participation from the schools. However there is need of continuous support in the form of seed material, monitoring, guidance etc.

What is the success of the project?

Good results were seen in 88 out of 100 schools.

Assessment and Future

*What are **challenges** what **barriers** do you face?*

1. *From the schools side* - schools require continuous guidance and monitoring which becomes difficult due to time, budget and human resource limitations. For participation and mainstreaming guidelines are required from the government department which is time consuming at times. Some times lack of motivation among the teachers becomes a barrier.
2. *In a macro context, the larger society* – Importance given to environment is not on par with the regular activities (either from the point of view of the donors, target group, bureaucratic systems, general community).

*What are the **facilitators**?*

Partnerships, finance

*What would you say where your **strengths** lie?*

Quality of the EE packages, result oriented programmes, intensive technical support and monitoring.

*Where are your **weaknesses**?*

Lack of sufficient human resource. Less publicity.

*What must **change**? What is needed therefore?*

Changes in strategy (e.g.: allotting more responsibilities to the government systems) towards ownership

*What are current **trends**, how will environmental activism look like in the future?*

It is positive picture now. The point is well taken and environment protection activities are welcome in the schools now. But as I mentioned before it requires intensive support from outside as the schools feel it difficult to integrate it in to the existing system. For e.g.: There are no separate gardeners, cleaners, etc. and these activities demands more time from teachers and students as well. This trend has to be changed and this should be treated as part of education and community partnerships should be explored for sustainability. Needless to say the encouragement from the department of education is a must.

A.5 Survey on schools and environment

Namaste! My name is Jenny Haberer. I'm a MA student from the Mudra Institute of Communication, Ahmedabad (MICA) and am working for the Indo-German Megacity project "Sustainable Hyderabad". The aim of the project is to make Hyderabad an environment friendly city by 2030. For the project I am conducting research in schools in Hyderabad on the topic of environmental awareness and eco-friendly behaviour.

By filling out this survey you will help me understand what is being done at your school in terms of climate change education and your knowledge, attitude and behaviour.

Please fill out the survey accurately and according to your true feelings. I will treat the information you give me confidentially, and will not share it with other people (e.g. your principal or teachers).

Age: _____ years   2. Tick Gender   or ☐   ☐

School name and location: _____

Our school is a private ☐ / government school ☐.   We follow: SSC ☐ CBSE ☐ / ICSE ☐ IB ☐

What is your mother tongue?

☐ Telugu   ☐ Urdu   ☐ Hindi   ☐ Kannada   ☐ Tamil   ☐ English   ☐ Other: _____

1. Is environmental education (EE) taught as a subject in your standard? Read options carefully and tick one:
   - ☐ Yes, **compulsory** subject.
   - ☐ Yes, **optional** subject and **I attend** it. Give reason:# _____
   - ☐ Yes, **optional** subject, but **I do not attend** it. Give reason: _____
   - ☐ No, **not taught as a subject.**

2. Have you **heard** of these **organizations** working for the environment? Tick the ones you know:
   - ☐ WWF (World Wide Fund for Nature)
   - ☐ NGC (National Green Corps)
   - ☐ CEE (Centre for Environment Education)
   - ☐ PEAS (Program for Environmental Awareness in Schools)
   - ☐ Greenpeace
   - ☐ IYCN (Indian Youth Climate Network)
   - ☐ L.U.G.T (Let's Unite for a Greener Tomorrow)#

   DID YOU KNOW?
   Many electric devices consume power even when switched off, sometimes as much power as when turned on!

   Write down any other you know that I have not mentioned: _____

3. Have you **attended** any **programs at your school** given by any of the organizations mentioned in question 2 (e.g. workshops, presentations, rallies, competitions)?   ☐ Yes   ☐ No

   If Yes Please write name(s) of organization(s) and program:

   Organization Name: _____   Program: _____
   Organization Name: _____   Program: _____

4. Are you an **active member** of any of the organizations? (E.g. in a club/youth group) Yes ☐ No ☐
   If Yes Please write name(s) of organization(s) and name of group/club:
   Organization Name: _____ Name of group/club: _____
   Organization Name: _____ Name of group/club: _____

5. Have you **heard/ read about** the following issues. Where have you heard/ read about them? Are you able to explain the meaning to others?

	Never heard	Read/ Heard	Where have you heard/ learned about it? (selecting more than one answer possible)						Can explain others
			School	Parent	Friend	Book	Media*¹	Organization*²	
Climate Change	☐	☐	☐	☐	☐	☐	☐	☐	☐
Global Warming	☐	☐	☐	☐	☐	☐	☐	☐	☐
Greenhouse gas (GHG) emissions have increased	☐	☐	☐	☐	☐	☐	☐	☐	☐
Increased CO_2 emission is causing global warming	☐	☐	☐	☐	☐	☐	☐	☐	☐
Ice caps/ glaciers are melting	☐	☐	☐	☐	☐	☐	☐	☐	☐
Sea levels are rising	☐	☐	☐	☐	☐	☐	☐	☐	☐
Recycling	☐	☐	☐	☐	☐	☐	☐	☐	☐
Fossil fuels are exhaustible natural resources	☐	☐	☐	☐	☐	☐	☐	☐	☐
Solar Energy	☐	☐	☐	☐	☐	☐	☐	☐	☐
Wind energy	☐	☐	☐	☐	☐	☐	☐	☐	☐
Composting	☐	☐	☐	☐	☐	☐	☐	☐	☐
Deforestation	☐	☐	☐	☐	☐	☐	☐	☐	☐
Rain water harvesting	☐	☐	☐	☐	☐	☐	☐	☐	☐

*¹ Note: Media could be TV, Radio, Magazine, Internet etc
*² Note: Organization refers to environment organizations I asked about in question above (e.g. WWF, NGC, etc.)

6. Tick **True (T) or False (F)** against the following statements:

   a) Clear, transparent water does not need purification and is always fit for drinking. ___
   b) A forest is a purifier of air and water. ___
   c) Compressed natural gas (CNG) is more polluting fuel than petrol. ___
   d) Fossil fuels are non-exhaustible natural resources. ___
   e) Only human interference causes waste in a forest. ___
   f) Climate change is a natural phenomenon. It is a change in long term weather patterns. ___
   g) Plastics and polythene bags have no impact on the fertility of soil. ___
   h) The discharge of waste water from homes, industries, hospitals, etc. into the river is pollution. ___
   i) An indiscriminate increase in the amount of greenhouse gases in the atmosphere can lead to excessive increase in the Earth's temperature leading to global warming. ___
   j) Compact fluorescent light bulbs save more energy than incandescent ones. ___

7. **What can you do** in everyday life to protect the environment?

_____   _____

_____   _____

_____   _____

8. Please mark the appropriate box to show **how you feel about** the following **statements**. Mark only one answer each line.

	Strongly agree	Agree	Neither agree nor disagree	Disagree	Strongly disagree
The quality of India's environment is getting worse.	☐	☐	☐	☐	☐
Climate change will have an effect on me and future generations.	☐	☐	☐	☐	☐
I am seriously concerned about problems climate change might bring.	☐	☐	☐	☐	☐
I want to help protect the environment, but don't know what to do.	☐	☐	☐	☐	☐
I think our school is environment friendly.	☐	☐	☐	☐	☐
I would like to learn more about the environment and climate change in school.	☐	☐	☐	☐	☐
Solving the problem is not my responsibility.	☐	☐	☐	☐	☐
After school I have many things to do and don't have time to do something for the environment.	☐	☐	☐	☐	☐
The government, industries and adults can do more than I, to solve the problem.	☐	☐	☐	☐	☐
Hands-on learning with experiments and activities helps me understand things better	☐	☐	☐	☐	☐
Environmental organizations are doing important work. They should do more with kids.	☐	☐	☐	☐	☐
I am willing to change my lifestyle to protect the environment	☐	☐	☐	☐	☐
Effects of climate change may decrease if we become more spiritual/ religious/ ethical.*!*	☐	☐	☐	☐	☐
All this green talk is simply a hype and the topic will pass soon	☐	☐	☐	☐	☐

9. In your opinion **what causes environment pollution**? Mention **three** things and give them ranking (1=strongest - 3=weakest)

Cause	Ranking
_____	_____
_____	_____
_____	_____

10. Please respond to the following by ticking **yes, no or don't know**:

	Yes	No	Don't know
Me and my family try to save **energy**	☐	☐	☐
We use alternative **energy** at home (solar energy, wind energy)	☐	☐	☐
We segregate our **waste** & reduce, reuse and recycle waste	☐	☐	☐
Sometimes, if there is no trash can/ bin I throw **waste** on the ground	☐	☐	☐
I have **planted** trees to help the environment	☐	☐	☐
I take care of a **plant** nursery	☐	☐	☐
We do rain**water** harvesting at home	☐	☐	☐
I **advice** others on how to be more environmental friendly, e.g. tell them if they do something that harms, pollutes the environment & how they can improve	☐	☐	☐

11. If you ticked **YES** in any of the categories in question 10, please **write a few words about it** (who told you to do it, how you do it, where, why, with whom, etc).

    Please give title to each category you're writing about: 'energy', 'waste', 'plantation', 'water', 'advice'

    _____
    _____
    _____
    _____
    _____
    _____

12. Please indicate **how you get to school** and back home?
    ☐ Walking ☐ School bus ☐ Public transport ☐ Bicycle
    ☐ Personal Car ☐ Car pool ☐ Two-wheeler ☐ Other: _____

13. What is your father's job? _____
14. What is your mother's job? _____
18. How many rooms are there in your home? _____ 19. How many people live in your home? _____
19. Where do you live? Independent House ☐ / Apartment Building ☐ / Pucca ☐ / Other:_____
20. Please tick the items you have at home:
    Fan☐ AC☐ Refrigerator☐ Bicycle☐ Car☐ Two-Wheeler☐ TV☐ Radio☐ Computer/Laptop☐

This is the end of the survey.

Finally please tell me how understandable the questions were to you?

   Very clear, I understood all questions
☐ I could understand nearly all questions
☐ Some questions were not clear to me, please specify:_____
☐ Totally unclear
☐ Other:_____

Please use this space for any comments you wish to leave:
_____
_____
_____
_____
_____
_____
_____

Thank you very much for your support!